Praise for *The Book of Natu*

Jacob Rodenburg's wealth of knowledge and infectious enthusiasm for nature make this a great resource for anyone wishing to stimulate children's connections with the natural world. The activities and games in the book are easy to replicate and it will be a boon to educators.

— Paul Elliott, professor, Trent School of Education, co-chair, Environmental and Sustainability Education in Teacher Education

What an incredibly handy and useful book! Jacob has had a hand in creating one of the most comprehensive community-based environmental programs in North America. Pathway to Stewardship and Kinship, a Peterborough, Ontario initiative, provides clear, developmentally savvy guidance on how to bond children with the natural world at all ages and stages. *The Book of Nature Connection* is the user's guide for making that connection happen. It's beautifully illustrated, clear as a bell, and joyous. Invaluable for classroom teachers, parents, and outdoor educators.

— David Sobel, environmental education leader, author, *Beyond Ecophobia: Reclaiming the Heart in Nature Education*

The Book of Nature Connection invites learners of all ages and abilities to experience the natural world in new and exciting ways. Enjoy this collection of games and tools that teach you to tune-in to your senses and connect with all your relations.

— Tegan Moss, executive director, Peterborough Green-Up Association

This beautiful compendium of nature activities is an essential bedside and backpack read for *all* educators—not just us nature nuts. Whether seeking future inspiration, or something to engage the group arriving in 15 minutes(!), this book provides an opportunity to grab-and-go or a deep dive. The best antidote to sensory anesthesia is to spend a day exploring your "neighbourwood" with Jacob. The second best is to explore his low-prop, high-impact activities, well-bundled to engage all the senses, including your sense of wonder!

— Karen O'Krafka, president, Council of Outdoor Educators of Ontario

The Book of Nature Connection will inspire and encourage you to see, hear, feel, touch, and connect (or re-connect) with the natural world in a more *senseful* way. Jacob has magically translated his wisdom and passion for outdoor education onto these pages, offering a unique collection of activities for all seasons, and all ages. This book is a much-needed resource at a time when we need nature as much as nature needs us. Fascinating, educational, playful, and thoughtful, *The Book of Nature Connection* is the ideal guide for teachers, parents, or anyone interested in discovering the wonder of nature.

— Lisa Nisbet, associate professor, Trent University,
co-creator, Nature Relatedness Scale,
author and researcher, natruerelatedness.ca

This is a wonderful resource for those who love to wander and learn from nature and for those who are novices at exploring the natural world! Jacob has revisioned some tried and true immersion experiences with a new twist. Flip to any page, read, and go outside for a new and refreshing way to experience wonder.

— Jennifer Seydel, executive director, Green Schools National Network

Jacob Rodenburg has crafted a must-read guide full of important information on how to reconnect with nature through practicing mindfulness and sensory activities. This is a great choice for anyone looking to unplug from our hectic, technology-dominated lives and be immersed in nature to reap the benefits!

— Aly Hyder Ali, urban nature organizer, Nature Canada

THE BOOK OF
NATURE CONNECTION

70 SENSORY ACTIVITIES
FOR ALL AGES

JACOB RODENBURG

new society
PUBLISHERS

Cover design by Diane McIntosh.
Image credits: p 3, 5, 7, 35, 67, 79, 93, 101, 109 © val_iva;
p 7, 35, 67, 79, 93 © Carlafcastagno; p 23, 77, 83 © SpicyTruffel;
p 51 © lily_calligrapher; p 105 © Darius SUL / Adobe Stock
Printed in Canada. First printing April 2022.

This book is intended to be educational and informative. It is not intended to serve as a guide. The author and publisher disclaim all responsibility for any liability, loss or risk that may be associated with the application of any of the contents of this book.

Inquiries regarding requests to reprint all or part of *The Book of Nature Connection* should be addressed to New Society Publishers at the address below.
To order directly from the publishers, please call 250-247-9737
or order online at www.newsociety.com

Any other inquiries can be directed by mail to:
New Society Publishers
P.O. Box 189, Gabriola Island, BC V0R 1X0, Canada
(250) 247-9737

LIBRARY AND ARCHIVES CANADA CATALOGUING IN PUBLICATION

Title: The book of nature connection : 70 sensory activities for all ages / Jacob Rodenburg.

Names: Rodenburg, Jacob, 1960– author.

Description: Includes index.

Identifiers: Canadiana (print) 20210336161 | Canadiana (ebook) 20210336188 |
ISBN 9780865719712 (softcover) | ISBN 9781550927658 (PDF) | ISBN 9781771423618 (EPUB)

Subjects: LCSH: Nature study—Activity programs. | LCSH: Natural history—Study and teaching—Activity programs. | LCSH: Natural history—Outdoor books. | LCGFT: Activity books.

Classification: LCC QH54.5 .R63 2022 | DDC 508—dc23

Funded by the Government of Canada | Financé par le gouvernement du Canada

Canada

New Society Publishers' mission is to publish books that contribute in fundamental ways to building an ecologically sustainable and just society, and to do so with the least possible impact on the environment, in a manner that models this vision.

new society PUBLISHERS

Certified B Corporation

FSC www.fsc.org | MIX Paper from responsible sources FSC® C016245

Contents

The Book of Nature Connection Worksheets are available for free download at:
https://newsociety.com/pages/book-of-nature-connection-worksheets

INTRODUCTION

STOP FOR ONE MOMENT. Cup your hands, squeeze your fingers together and slip them behind your ears. Now push your ears forward. Notice how much better you can hear? Now listen. Really listen. What do you hear? Do you hear the rustling of paper, music playing in the background, the creaking of a chair, or a car driving by? How many different sounds can you notice at any one time?

Credit: iStock.

Cupping your ears helps you hear better.

OUR SENSES

We humans have the capacity to sense the world in amazing ways. Our environment is a delightfully textured tapestry of sound, sight, taste, feel, and smell. Humans have evolved to deeply sense the world around us. Our senses of hearing, sight, taste, feeling, and smell are adaptations that have enabled us to survive for thousands upon thousands of years. They've helped us identify safe food to eat (by smell and taste), they've protected us from danger (seeing and hearing pred-

ators), and they've helped us deal with discomfort (our bodies signal when we in pain, or if we are too cold or too hot).

Each of our senses is a remarkable evolutionary achievement. For example, our small protruding ears help us to pick up a range of sound vibrations. We have hearing that is sensitive enough to detect wind gently moving through grasses and bold enough to deal with the lusty screams of a toddler in the full throws of a tantrum. We hear sounds

1

from many locations simultaneously—one could say we hear in three dimensions, in complete surround sound.

The same holds true for our vision. Right now, move your head slowly from side to side. Look around you—all the way around. Notice the incredible shades of colors, the sheen of light reflecting off a table, the subtle texture on paper, and the bold lines of ink on this text. Flick your eyes off into the distance and now to something very close by. Notice that you, too, have the eyes of a predator—stereoscopic vision that is able to perceive objects in three dimensions. You can gauge both depth and position. With help of special cones in the back of our eyes, you can distinguish between one million

distinct shades of color. Or if you are lucky enough to be one of those rare tetrachromats (having the ability to see four distinct primary colors instead of the normal three), you may be able to distinguish between 100 million different shades!

Rub your thumb across the tips of your fingers. Feel the ridges of skin that encase them. We are enveloped in skin—the barrier between us and the world—and special receptors called Meissner's corpuscles (in our finger tips, we have over 9,000 of these per square inch) respond to the slightest pressure, a gentle caress or the sweep of a cool breeze.

Take one large breath and focus on the smell of the air around you. With every

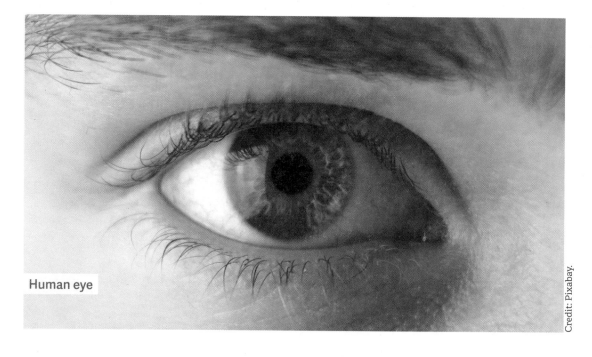

Human eye

Credit: Pixabay.

breath in and out, we pick up odors—the latest research suggests we can detect millions of them. Smell is one of our most evocative senses. With a whiff of freshly baked bread and spring rain, we can be transported back to our grandmother's kitchen or recall how, as a child, we stomped—rubber booted—in muddy puddles under an April shower.

Rub your tongue across the roof of your mouth. Can you feel the texture of your taste buds? Crammed in our mouth and shaped like tiny volcanoes, our more than 10,000 taste buds help us to detect the faintest of flavors; for example, our tongue can help us detect bitterness in as little as 1 part per 2 million. Sophisticated sommeliers (wine connoisseurs) can tell what region grapes from a fine red wine were grown in after just a few small sips. They draw on a wide palette of poetic phrases to describe the taste, color, and bouquet of different wines. Wines might be lean, restrained, silky, foxy, or crunchy.

It raises the question, can we become nature sommeliers? Perhaps we can practice drinking the natural world in through all of our senses. Can we savor the natural world with the same kind of attentiveness as a sommelier? One wonders how we might cultivate *sensefulness*, a full-bodied connection to the world around us.

In our modern technologically saturated world, we really only have time to use two of our senses, namely, our sense of sight and

our sense of hearing. In fact, most of the way we experience the world today is squeezed into two dimensions and confined to a flat and glowing screen. In North America, the average child spends close to 7 hours and 50 minutes in front of devices per day. Astonishingly, adults can spend more than 10 hours a day on screen time, and this number is steadily growing.

We somehow think that life is more complete when we are connected to our devices. It is true, our smart phones, tablets, and computers help us to discover the world in new ways. We instantly get in touch with our friends overseas; we can search out tidbits of information in fractions of a second. And while we feel connection to our friends virtually, we also recognize that something is missing. We see their ghosted image but not their full selves. We miss their touch; we miss their subtle odor. We miss the fact that we are sharing the same air, the same place, and the same moment in all of its immediacy. With the sheer amount of time spent in front of screens, we tend to forget that nature has graced us with these marvelous sensory abilities—senses that enable us to connect to the world around us in a deep and abiding way. And in a way that technology simply cannot replicate.

Perhaps we intuitively know this, but mounting

evidence suggests that time spent in nature enhances our physical and mental health. Just breathing in forest air strengthens our immune system. Simply seeing the color green releases serotonin, the feel-good hormone. Time spent in nature helps us to focus better, improves our sleep, and boosts our mood and energy levels. In a world where more than half of us live in urban areas, now, more than ever, we need nature.

I hope this book will encourage you, your families, your neighbors, your students, and your friends to take the time to unplug from technology and plug in to nature through the wonder of your senses. I also hope these sensory activities will inspire you to immerse yourself in the natural world in both new and refreshing ways. Think about your senses as "nature's pipeline"—your most direct connection to the natural systems that sustain us all. To soak the world in through all of our senses takes practice, mindfulness, and deliberation. Some people have argued that in today's modern world, our children are suffering from a measure of *sensory anesthesia*, a dulling of their senses. Remember this, with time spent in nature with all of our senses awakened and primed, we feel more alive and more in tune with the world around us. Could it be that we,

Nature connection

Credit: Pixabay.

along with our children, are feeling a sense of loneliness and alienation because we feel disconnected from the very life systems that nurture and sustain us all? By immersing ourselves and our children again and again in natural spaces, we'll come to cherish them, not simply as places to go, but as places that we belong to. And in belonging, we feel more complete.

It is my hope that you'll come to imagine these places as an integral part of your community—as part of your "neighborwood." The Anishinaabe First Nations use the phrase *Nwiikaanigana*, meaning "all my relations," to express their sense of connection to the land, air, water, plants, and animals around them. May we all come to view the natural world around us in this fulsome way.

STEVE VAN MATRE

The founder of the Earth Education movement, Steve Van Matre, is an extraordinary outdoor educator. He believes that children will become more environmentally engaged if they understand the ecological principles that govern the natural world and if they are given the opportunity to activate all their senses as well. Back in the 1970s, Van Matre was concerned that nature educators focused too much on naming and relaying information in an encyclopedic manner. Along with developing innovative approaches to outdoor education including Earth Keepers and Sunship Earth, Van Matre conceived a number of sensory awareness activities that helped children appreciate and savor the natural world. He called these *acclimatization activities*. From swamp walks to basement windows, from micro-trails to picture frames, Van Matre's creative approach to sensory awareness is the inspiration for this book, and a number of his activities can be found among these pages.

MINDFULNESS AND NATURE

Mindfulness is the deliberate practice of tuning into your feelings and what your body is experiencing as you connect to the world around you. It means letting go of your thoughts and focusing on the here and now. For example, standing in a pool of sunlight and feeling the sensation of the sun's rays against your face. You might pay attention to the wind brushing against your cheek and the faint scent of pine in the air. You might imagine the earth pulsing with life beneath your feet. It is about being fully present and open to this moment and all the gifts that this moment brings. The natural world is a place of constant change, of resiliency and renewal. By opening up all your senses and allowing the natural world to wash over you, you feel refreshed and awakened. The clutter and stress of all the things your mind is telling you that you need to do and accomplish in your daily life begins to recede. You feel a sense of rootedness to something larger than yourself. The act of drawing yourself out of yourself and into the world around you helps you to cultivate and enhance empathy.

Studies have shown that our brains function differently while in nature. We relax more, and this increases alpha wave activity that helps us to feel calmer. Meanwhile, activity in our frontal lobe, the part that is responsible for executive function and analytic thought, decreases. We feel less stress, calmer, and more at peace.

Here are some hints for practicing mindfulness in nature:

- Find a quiet spot in a place that is as natural as you can access. If you live in a large city, go to a nearby park. If you are able to get away from the sounds of city life, so much better.
- Stand, sit, or even lie down.
- Start by tuning into the sounds you can hear. If thoughts come rushing over you, try not to react to them. Instead focus on the sensations of this time and this place.
- Breathe slowly in through your nose and gently exhale through your mouth or nose. Smell the air. Can you detect a hint of earthiness, of moisture in the air, the scent of trees and leaves?
- Gently caress the earth, the grass, a stick, or leaves. Concentrate on the sensation that this makes on the tips of your fingers. What is its texture? Rub some soil between your fingers. Feel its coolness and freshness.
- Look around and attend to the various colors. What hues do you notice? How many shades of green, gray, brown can you observe? Look up, notice the color of the sky: is it the same shade of blue, white, or gray? Watch clouds and the textures, patterns, and shapes they make.
- You can practice mindfulness even as you walk. While walking, focus on the sounds your feet make as you move. Practice all-around watching, not just looking at your feet. Try widening your field of vision. Feel the sensation of your body balancing as you move across different terrains. Focus on the sounds around you. Where are they coming from? Notice the very slight temperature change as you move from forest to field or from a sun-washed area to shade.
- It is a wonderful law of physics that no two people can occupy the same space at the same time. You are the only one to be in this space, at this time. Your view of the world is completely unique. Celebrate this beautiful perspective that you and only you are privileged to be part of.
- **A word of caution, in the book we have suggested activities that call for the mindful harvesting of small bits of nature. Be aware that in Parks and Conservation Areas, harvesting from nature is prohibited. If this isn't your land, always ask permission before you take anything from the natural world. On your own land, you might even ask the plant itself for permission.**

NATURAL SOUNDS

WHEN WE HEAR, what do we hear? If you were able to float in space and listen to the surrounding universe you would hear…well, absolutely nothing. That is because sound needs something to move through, a medium. Here on Earth, the sound we hear travels through air. When you clap your hands together, you create a series of airwaves, just like a pebble causes waves when dropped in a pond. When these airwaves travel into your ear (also having the interesting name of pinnae), they are funnelled into your ear canal. Deep inside your ear canal, your eardrum begins to vibrate. And when your eardrum vibrates, it causes a series of tiny interconnected bones to move (the ossicles: malleus, incus, and stapes). The last bone, the stapes, transfers the sound vibrations to the cochlea. The cochlea is a snail-shaped sac filled with fluid and lined with tiny hairs. These hairs are so sensitive that they respond to different pitches or frequencies of sound. Each tiny hair generates a nerve impulse that stimulates the auditory nerve, and the impulse travels to the hearing centers of our brain. Our brain then translates this into sound. While it sounds (ha) like it might take a long time for all of this to happen, from when the first sound waves enter our ear to when we actually register sound just takes a mere fraction of a second.

SOUND CATCHERS

If you've ever closely watched a deer, you'll notice how its large ears are always twitching and moving. Other animals too, from rabbits to foxes, are continually using their ears to focus in on sound. As an animal, hearing movement helps you to either escape danger or to catch your prey. Your survival depends upon it.

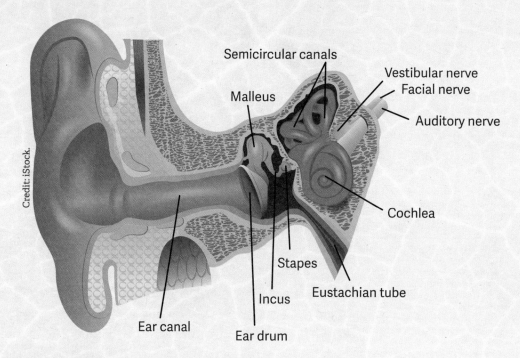

Credit: iStock.

Semicircular canals

Malleus

Vestibular nerve
Facial nerve

Auditory nerve

Cochlea

Stapes

Eustachian tube

Incus

Ear canal

Ear drum

Deer Ears

Here's how you too can turn your ears into deer ears.

- Press your fingers together and cup your hands. Place them directly behind your ears and push forward. You can amplify your hearing by as much as ten times by using this technique.
- Now find a quiet spot. Close your eyes and listen to the natural sounds that surround you. Perhaps it is the swish of grass, the gurgle of water, the gentle murmur of tree leaves, or the creaking of branches. How many natural sounds can you hear? There are people who have claimed to hear caterpillars chewing. Is that you?

Extenda-Ears

What if you could make a device to extend your ears to help you hear better? Here is a simple and quick sound collector that really works.

- Roll one large piece of paper into a cone shape, keeping one end as large as you can and the other small enough to fit into your ear and secure with tape.
- Place the narrow end of the cone to your ear but be careful not to go directly inside your ear!
- Go outside and listen to any natural sounds. Can you hear any better? The funnel focuses vibrations into our ear canal, amplifying sound.

Jacob's Homemade Sound Catchers

- Cut out a cardboard paper plate (or card stock) into an ear shape so it fits along the side of your head and behind your ears.
- Make two holes. Slip a dowel or stick inside the holes as shown in the photo and curl the card stock. Secure with tape. And voilà: instant sound catchers.

Try them out and maybe you can hear some secrets being told from across the room.

Homemade sound catchers

Credit: Jacob Rodenburg.

LEARNING FROM BATS

Humans can hear from 20 to 20,000 hertz (a measurement of sound wave frequency). One hertz equals one sound wave over one second. Many animals can hear way beyond the frequencies that humans can hear. Take for example bats. As a way to navigate in the dark and to hunt, bats send out a stream of high-pitched sounds called "ultrasounds" at intervals of 10 to 20 per second and then listen as they bounce back. Bats create a kind of picture of their environment by tracking sound. Most people think that bats are blind—they aren't; they just do most of their hunting in the dark using their remarkable sonar capabilities. Dolphins and whales use this same technique to hunt underwater. Submarines create computer-generated maps of the seafloor by sending out sound pulses.

It turns out that some humans can activate this ability as well. Daniel Kish is completely blind. Yet he can navigate through the busy streets of Long Beach, California, and find his way back home again. How does he do it? Just like a bat, he sends out a series of clicks by moving his tongue against his cheeks and listens for the sound to return. He says he can create a three-dimensional mental image of his environment, sketched by sound with "depth, character, and richness." Over the years, he has become so good at seeing the world through sound that he regularly hikes alone in the mountains, cooks his own meals, and even rides his bike through his suburban neighborhood. Let's think about David as we try out some of these sound activities. Does that "sound" good to you?

Credit: Pixabay.

Sound Claps

- Go outside and find a place (if you can) where there are bushes, trees, boulders, even buildings.
- Turn one direction and clap loudly. Listen to the quality of the sound returning. Now stand directly in front of an object (say a large tree or a wall) and clap in exactly the same way again. Did you notice how the quality of the sound changed?
- Try closing your eyes. Experiment in front of different natural objects and try to "see" the sound as it bounces back. Can you create a three-dimensional image? How does it compare to the actual image you see in front of you?
- Practice in front of various natural objects (a bush, a large tree, a small tree, a boulder). Does your sound image become progressively clearer, the more you practice?

Click Paths

For this activity, you'll need a blindfold, a straight pathway through the woods, and a friend. Can you navigate the world like Daniel Kish does? Let's see (or hear, in this case)!

- Find a clear and flat pathway through the woods. Make sure it is fairly straight and clear of obstructions (roots, rocks, holes, cracks) for about 150 feet (50 meters) or so. Now walk the path a few times, noting natural objects along the way from both directions. Perhaps you'll notice that big white pine back from the edge of the path or the sprawling lilac bush or that hill in the distance.
- Now walk the pathway again, this time making clicking noises just like Daniel does by moving your tongue against or cheek or teeth (whatever works best for you). Practice clicking as you walk along really concentrating on the sound. Can you hear it subtly change as you pass by different natural objects?
- Here is where your friend comes in handy. Have a friend stand at the end of the 150 feet (50 meters) path. Let them know to warn you if you are going to stray from the path and run into something painful.
- Place the blindfold around your eyes and slowly walk the path, clicking as you go. Did the sound help you navigate? Practice a few times and let your friend have a turn as well. Were you able to create a sound map just like Daniel Kish? Did the sound picture in your mind bear any resemblance to the trail you could actually see?

Bat and Moth

Remember how bats hunt by sending out a stream of high-pitched sonar waves that help the bat echolocate their food? This game does a wonderful job of replicating how sonar helps bats to pinpoint the exact location of their food when they are flying at night.

Here is a tried-and-true game based on that childhood staple Marco Polo. You'll need a group of 12 or more, at least two blindfolds, and an open area.

- Select one volunteer to be a bat and another to be a moth. Have everyone else make a large circle facing inward. Their arms should be stretched out so that their hands, when extended, are about half a meter from the person to next to them. These folks will serve as your "cave walls."
- Blindfold both the bat and the moth. Explain that it is now dark outside and neither of the bat nor the moth can see very well. In this game, the bat's job is to "catch" the moth.
- In real life, a bat would send out a series of high-pitched sounds and listen for the sound's return—zeroing in on the moth. When located, they would then either scoop out the moth with their tail just like a catcher's

mitt and transfer it to their mouth, or they would smack the moth with their wing to transfer it to their tail and subsequently into their mouth. Incidentally, a single bat can eat up to 1,200 mosquitoes in one hour and up to 8,000 in one night!

- To show how echolocation works, have the bat say distinctly "bat" loudly and clearly. Every time the moth hears the bat say "bat," it must say equally loudly and clearly "moth" (to show how the sonar pulse is being reflected back to the bat). If either the bat or the moth ventures too closely to the cave walls, have the walls gently say "wall," so there aren't any collisions.
- Now ask the bat to try to tag the moth. After a short while, ask the bat to experiment by increasing the frequency of their call. Does this help them track the moth more effectively?
- If you like, add another moth to the game. Some moths have evolved to start evasive manoeuvres if they hear a bat's sonar. They'll begin dive-rolling and zigzagging, trying to move in an abrupt and unpredictable fashion. Can the moth try some evasive moves to confuse the bat? Some species of

tiger moths have evolved to jam the bat's sonar by making a series of disruptive clicks using a special organ in their thorax called a tymbal.
- Biologists have called the bat/moth predator/prey relationship a kind of arms race as each evolve ever more complex methods to catch prey and to avoid being eaten.

Be a Bat Detector

- Purchase a bat detector. There are a number that are available, starting at about $50. They take the high-pitched tones that bats emit and turn them into sounds that humans can hear. Using the bat detector, you can get an idea of what species of bat might be active by tuning into the specific frequency that bat uses to catch its prey.
- Find a place where bats hang out: a barn, a forest with mature trees, a city park, or perhaps the roof of an old house. Make sure you arrive shortly before dusk. Hold the detector aloft and adjust the frequency of the detector so that you can hear bats make their distinctive clicking sound. Start at 45 hertz and adjust up or down accordingly. Note the bat detector can help you differentiate between some species based on the frequency of their sonar.
- If you hone in on a bat, note how the clicks accelerate as it hones in on its prey. Report your findings to citizen science sites such as iNaturalist or Neighborwood Bat Watch.

Bat Frequency Chart	
Species of bat	**Frequency range**
Eastern small footed bat	40–50 kHz
Little brown bat	40–48 kHz
Northern long-eared bat	40–55 kHz
Silver bat	22–30 kHz
Tri-colored bat	40–48 kHz
Big brown bat	30–38 kHz
Red bat	35–45 kHz
Hoary bat	20–25 kHz

LISTENING TO OTHER ANIMALS AND TREES

Tree Songs

Here is a wonderful word for you during your next game of Scrabble: *psithurism*, meaning the whispering of wind as it blows through trees and rustles leaves. Did you know that you can get close to identifying the type of tree by listening to the quality the sound of the wind makes as it moves through the tree tops? Perhaps you have this ability?

- To find out, see if you can locate a white pine tree. You can tell it is a white pine by its long soft needles (always in bunches of five). One way to remember is that there are five letters in "white" and five bundled needles on a white pine tree.
- Sit beneath its branches and focus in on the sweeping sound of the wind.

There is a soft whooshing sound that is characteristic of pines. Oaks and maples have more of a chattering quality as the leaves rustle against one another. Quaking aspens shiver and bushes whisper.

- Take a note pad and describe the quality of sound you hear for each type of tree you visit. Try to remember these distinctive sounds. Use a field guide or an app such as PlantSnap to help you identify the trees that you don't know.
- On a windy day, savor the wind's symphony of soft music that strums the leaves and plucks the branches of nearby trees. In nature, there is music everywhere, if we take the time to stop, listen and enjoy.

Tree songs

Credit: iStock.

Heartbeat of a Tree

We forget that those tall trees that form the backdrop of our city parks and school grounds are pulsing with life! In the spring, sap rises from the roots up through the trunk to the tips of every branch. The energy from the sap helps leaves to form. Just like listening to your own heartbeat, you can hear the gurgling, crackling, sputtering of the sap as it moves up the trunk. Early spring is the best time, when the sap is just starting to rise. Hardwoods tend to be a better choice than softwoods.

- To listen to the sap rising, select maples, birches, or cherry trees.
- Find one that is more than 6 inches in diameter but not too large (if the bark is too thick, you'll be less likely to hear anything).
- You'll need a stethoscope, which you can purchase online or you can find used ones for $30 or so.

- Place the bell of the stethoscope against the trunk and be very still. You may need to move the bell around until you find a spot where you can hear the best. Enjoy the exuberant sounds of a tree waking up after a long winter's nap!

Heartbeat of a tree

Credit: iStock.

Bird Whispering

I was skeptical when a friend said he could call birds in from the forest. "What are you talking about?" I asked. Birds are shy. If there is one thing I know, they don't come when they're called.

With a smile on his face and a glint his eye, he said "I'll show you."

We stood under the canopy of oaks and maples, when he tilted his head upwards and let go with the strangest of sounds. By pursuing his lips, he uttered a stream of loud "pssshhhing" noises. He repeated each phrase a few times a second (pish, pish, pish), emphasizing the P and the "ish" parts. I looked at him quizzically. Then he began to kiss the back of his hand. What the heck? I thought; surely he needs some psychological attention. Then he told me to stand still. So I did.

It was then that the birds began to arrive. First black-capped chickadees flitted in, soon followed by white- and red-breasted nuthatches. Warblers, woodpeckers, and even other birds swooped by to check us out. After a few minutes, we had over sixty birds near us. Some of the chickadees were only a few feet away! How did my friend do this?

He used the secret weapon known to birders as "pishing." It works especially well with small songbirds. Pishing simply involves taking a deep breath and quickly repeating the sound "pissh" as you let the air out in one drawn-out exhale. Try to pish yourself. Yes, people may look at you strangely, but you'll gain their admiration when birds start to arrive.

- If you are in a forested area where you hear the sound of a chickadee (with their distinctive "chick-a-dee, chick-a-dee" call), then stand next to a tree that has lots of branches. Chickadees feel safer when there is plenty of cover.
- Stay very still and begin pishing. At first, pish fairly loudly every few seconds. Continue this for at least a couple of minutes and then lower the

Black-capped chickadee

Credit: Pixabay.

volume when birds start to arrive. You can also kiss the back of your hand or fingers, creating squealing noises. Chickadees and nuthatches are especially receptive to both of these sounds, but other species will almost always show up, especially if you are patient. Don't be surprised if you end up with birds practically at arm's reach.

- It is believed that birds respond to pishing because it sounds similar to the scold calls of chickadees, which are used when there is a potential threat in the area, such as an owl. Other chickadees, along with birds of other species, are attracted by these sounds because they are curious about the nature of the potential threat.
- You can pish birds in during each of the seasons, pishing seems to work best during the fall and winter.

Bird Mnemonics

There are few things more beautiful than the ethereal sound of a wood thrush's song rising and falling on a mist-filled morning or hearing the call of a loon echoing across a granite-rimmed lake. Each bird species has a unique sound. Birds make vocalizations in a special organ called a syrinx, located deeper in their throat than a human larynx, which can produce quite loud vocalizations for their size. Some birds can even make two sounds at once. For example, a veery can sing in harmony with itself.

There is something so comforting about walking in a forest and being able to recognize the calls and songs of bird species. In a way, you are among friends. Just like hearing a friend's voice, you become familiar with each unique sound. And you don't have to see a bird to know that it is there.

You can get to know your bird vocalizations. To start with, there is a difference between a bird's song and call. Songs are made in the spring, almost exclusively by males. Translating from Bird to English, songs say: "Hey if you are girl bird of my kind, I'm over here! Or if you are another male, back off! This is my part of the forest." Calls, on the other hand, are more about contact and alarm—males and females touching base or uttering a warning that danger is near. The sentinel of the forest, the blue jay often squawks a loud "jay, jay, jay" call if a hawk or an owl is nearby. A black-capped chickadee uses its iconic "chicka-dee-dee-dee" call to stay in touch with its flock during the fall and winter. But its song may be less familiar. In the spring, the male chickadee lifts its beak skyward and lets out a slurred three-syllable whistle that sounds like "Hey sweetie!"

Perhaps this will sound familiar. Does the plaintive sound of a mourning dove sound like "There's nothing to do"? Or is the northern cardinal reminiscent of "Cheer, cheer, cheer, party, party"? Of course, they are not really saying those things. It is just the rhythm, cadence, and arrangement of notes that bring to mind these sayings. These mnemonic (or memory) devices are simply a handy way for us to recognize these unique songs and calls.

Below you'll find some tried-and-true

Bird Mnemonic Chart

Name of bird	Suggested mnemonic
American robin	Cheer-a-lee, cheer-up, cheer-a-lee
Red-winged blackbird	Konk-er-me
Common yellowthroat	Witchity-witchity-witchity-witch
White-breasted nuthatch	Wee-wee-wee-wee-wee-wee
Northern cardinal	Cheer, cheer, cheer, party, party
Mourning dove	There is nothing to do!
Yellow warbler	Sweet-sweet-sweet-I'm so sweet
Black capped chickadee	Hey sweetie
Song sparrow	Maids maids bring out your tea kettle-ettle-ettle
Great horned owl	Who's awake? Me too!
Barred owl	Who cooks for you, who cooks for you, who cooks for you all?
American goldfinch	Pa-chip-chip-chip – a chip for me
American bittern	Gulp a pump
Baltimore oriole	Here; here; come right here; dear
Blue jay	Jay-jay-jay & queedle-queedle-queedle
Eastern meadowlark	Spring of the year

mnemonics for common bird species. Bird apps such as Sibley Birds or Larkwire will also help you identify bird calls and songs. Song Sleuth will even help you ID a bird song recorded by your phone. Go out into the forest and, using your cupped ears, really listen. Using a pad and pen, try to develop a saying to help you remember the song or call. You can also use Peterson's *Field Guide to Bird Song* to help you learn the vocalizations of a variety of bird species in your area. Bird apps such as Sibley Birds or Larkwire will also help you identify bird calls and songs. Start by learning a dozen or so of the common ones and each spring add a few more to your repertoire.

Get to Know Your Frog Songs

And yes, frogs sing too! And they sing for the same reason birds do. The males are trying to attract a mate, and they also are fighting for territory. Walk to a nearby marsh, swamp or bog in early spring, just as the sun is starting to set. Remember to slip on your deer ears. Listen for the high piercing peep of a spring peeper or maybe the trilling bursts of sound from the chorus frog. You might also hear the low garomph of the bullfrog or the throaty croak of the leopard frog. Some species call earlier during spring, some later. During the day, you might even hear the birdlike trill of the gray tree frog, depending on where you live. To learn to identify the frog songs in your province or state, go to frogwatch.ca (Canada) or aza.org/frogwatch/ (US)

Bullfrog

Credit: Pixabay.

Frog Songs

FROG SPECIES	SOUND	WHEN THEY SING
Spring peeper	High peep peep sound	Early spring
American bullfrog	Deep, resonant "rr-uum" or "jug-o-rum"	Late spring/early summer
Wood frog	Sounds like a quaking duck	Early spring
Green frog	"gulp, gulp" deep from the throat	Late spring/early summer
Leopard frog	A throaty ahhhhhhhhhh…	Early spring
Chorus frog	Short bursts of trills made with your lips or tongue	Mid- to late spring
Eastern cricket frog	Use your tongue to make "click-click-click"-like sounds. Reminiscent of pebbles clicked together; cricket-like	Late spring/early summer
Gray tree frog	Slow musical bird-like trill lasting 2 to 3 seconds. Use your lips or tongue	Late spring/early summer
Fowler's toad	Nasal, sheep-like "waaaaa"	Late spring/early summer
American toad	A sustained trill from lips or throat	Early to late spring
Western toad	Soft, quickly repeated "peep-peep"	Late winter/early spring
Great Basin spadefoot toad	Short harsh nasal-sounding snores at 1 second intervals	Late spring/early summer
Great Plains toad	Rapidly repeated, harsh, machine gun-like trill; 20–30 sec's in length	Late spring/mid-summer
Plains Spadefoot toad	Short, harsh, barks (ouak-ouak) at 1 second intervals	Late spring/early summer
Pacific tree frog	"Kreck-ek, Kreck-ek, Kreck-ek"	Late winter/late spring
Red-legged frog	Weak series of 5–7 notes lasting 1–3 seconds "uh-uh-uh-uh-uh"	Late winter/early summer
Sierran tree frog	"Rib-it", or "krek-ek", with the last syllable rising in inflection	Nov–July (depending on location)

Nature Spectrograph

A spectrograph is a visual picture of sound. Here is a way that you really can focus on the quality and loudness of the natural sounds around you. You'll need a pad of paper and pencil for this activity.

- Draw a simple graph (see right). On the left side, make an arrow indicating how loud the sound is: higher up the page means louder, lower down softer. The axis on bottom of the page indicates how long the sound lasts.
- Pick one sound. Perhaps it is a robin calling. Does your sound steadily rise, does it curve upward, or does it trill? Try to depict the sound on the spectrograph.
- Use your spectrograph to focus on a few other natural sounds. Several days later, can you remember the sound by reading the spectrograph?

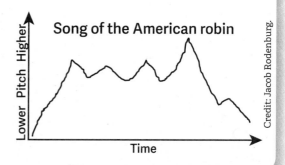

Song of the American robin

Lower Pitch Higher

Time

Credit: Jacob Rodenburg.

Fingers Up

Here is a simple game that helps you concentrate on the different sounds in nature.

- Ask your participants to sit down and squeeze their eyes shut. Every time they hear a distinctive natural sound, have them lift a finger. With each additional sound, have them lift one more finger.
- After a few minutes, ask participants to open their eyes and reveal how many sounds they heard. What did they think they were?

Make an Acorn Whistle

Here is an evocative sound produced by something children love to find. We know that oaks produce acorns each year. What is less known is that every 5 or 6 years, red and white oaks produce a massive amount of acorns—as many as 10 times the number in a typical year. This is called a "mast" year—scientists believe that this abundance of nuts helps to ensure that at least some of the acorns will grow into trees. Is this a mast year?

- Visit your local park or nearby forest and look around. Find an oak tree (most oak leaves have rounded or pointy lobes, see page 67).
- Hunt for an acorn and remove the cap. Take the cap and place your thumbs over the hollow in a V shape (see photo). Bend your thumbs slightly.

- Blow across your knuckles and over the hollow. You should hear a sharp whistling sound. If you don't, shift your thumbs around until you hear a clear whistle. Watch out for incoming dogs!

Credit: Jacob Rodenburg.

Woodpeckers

Think about it… Woodpeckers slam their heads with a force of more than 1,000 times of gravity against tree trunks, using their sharp beaks to excavate a hole and find insects. How is it that they don't get brain damage, or at the very least a headache? It turns out that they have specially reinforced skulls and extra muscles in their necks. In fact, some woodpeckers have a tongue that is so long (several times the length of its beak) that, when not in use, it is wrapped around the back of their skull. During the spring, male woodpeckers will drum (also known as tapping or tattooing) as a way to attract a mate and establish his territory. Using a resonant object such as a dead and hollow tree or stump or log and even aluminum gutters, they create a distinctive pattern of rapidly repeating sounds. Different woodpeckers create different drumming patterns.

Woodpecker Drumming Game

Play this game in a large open wooded area. A city park will work well.

- You'll need 2 dowels (¾" in diameter and about 18" long) or 2 thick sticks, enough for half the participants.
- Hand out copies of the woodpecker cards on the next page. Make sure these are paired up (for example, two hairy woodpecker cards, two sapsucker cards). Each pair should have one participant with the sticks and one without the sticks (but each should have the same card).
- On a given signal, the participant with the sticks runs and hides. They begin using their sticks to drum the pattern that is indicated on their card. They represent the male woodpecker of that species. The other, the female, is listening for the correct pattern. Can she find her species by sound alone? With everyone drumming at the same time, it can be a bit of a challenge! Give it a try.

Woodpecker Drumming Game

Hairy woodpecker

As quick and as fast as you can for about 5 seconds—rapid, even beats—pause for 10 seconds—resume. A real hairy woodpecker can drum 25 times per second!

Pileated woodpecker

Slow and resonate, rolling taps that lasts for 5 seconds or so and then begins again. The pattern is somewhat like knocking on a door.

Sapsucker

Slower, morse code like taps. Something like tap tap, tapity tap, tap, tap tapity tap. Some slow, some faster.

Downy woodpecker

Fast taps for about 2 seconds, then stop for 3 seconds and the resume.

Credit: Pixabay.

Trunk Sounds

Sound travels differently through different densities of wood.

- Using the dowels or sticks from the last activity, have someone stand on the backside of a trunk of a hardwood (such as a maple or oak) and place their ear against the trunk. Have someone tap the tree using their dowel or stick from the other side.
- Move to a softer wood such as a cedar, pine, or hemlock. Try out different diameters of trunks. Is the difference in the quality of sound between hardwoods and softwoods, between thicker and thinner trunks? Is it possible to distinguish between different species?
- If you find a long trunk lying on the forest floor, carefully place your ear along the thinner end and ask another person on the stouter end to create small knocking sounds or rubbing sounds with your dowel. Does the sound carry along the trunk? Birds can often hear the scrabbling of claws far below as an animal begins to climb the tree, helping to alert them that danger is coming!

Trunk knocking

Credit: Jacob Rodenburg.

STALKING GAMES

Here are a few games that help you move through the woods silently and mindfully. Stalking, or quiet walking, takes a bit of practice, but once you've mastered this, you'll hear so much more than on a careless plod through the woods. Our ancestors and Indigenous people from all over the world learned to stalk prey in order to get as close as possible for a successful hunt.

Individual Game

- Place your hands on your knees and crouch just a bit. By taking this position, you can freeze during any part of your walk. Rest the weight of your body on your back leg. Now take a small step and ease your weight onto the toes of your front foot. Make sure there are no crunchy leaves or dried sticks before you commit your entire weight.
- Transfer all your weight on those toes and roll along the outside of your foot and onto your heel. Do the same with the other foot. Take small and deliberate steps. A good stalker will take a long time to move 150 feet (50 meters)—but they won't make a single noise.
- Practice on a variety of natural surfaces: a grassy field, a forest floor, and a stony path. Once you have the hang of this, try the following stalking games.

Group Stalking Game (for 5 participants or more)

- Have two volunteers crouch on the ground, blindfolded, facing each other, about 5 meters (15 feet) apart.
- One at a time, challenge your participants to stalk quietly in between the blindfolded volunteers. If the volunteers hear a sound, they should point to exactly where the sound is coming from. If they point directly at a participant, that person must sit down.
- How many participants can successfully stalk past the two volunteers?

Here's a variation on this game:

- Form a large circle facing inward about 30 to 45 feet (10 to 15 meters) or so. Have a volunteer sit in the middle. Blindfold them and place a number of sticks (Popsicle sticks will do nicely) in front of and beside the participant (enough for all the people in the circle).
- Instruct the participants on the outside of the circle to see if they can stalk and grab a stick. The volunteer in the middle points if they hear a sound. If they point directly at stalker, that person must return to the circle. How many can successfully steal a stick?

Drum Stalking

You'll need a drum or two sticks that when clacked together make a loud sound.

- Have a volunteer (prey) hide in the woods nearby. Participants (hunters) try to catch the volunteer by touching them.
- The volunteer must make a thump on their drum or with their sticks every 10 seconds or so. They are free to move about. Participants use sound of the drum/sticks to locate their prey. If the volunteer sees someone coming, they point and that person must move 15 feet (5 meters) away. Will there be a successful hunt?

Stalking games

Credit: Jacob Rodenburg.

Sound Makers

Materials in nature have their own distinctive sounds. As you walk, think about the different sounds the crunch of leaves or the squelch of mud or the squeak of snow make underfoot. Here is a quick game to help you appreciate how different natural sounds can be.

- Find small containers with lids (small yogurt containers will do nicely), blindfolds, a variety of natural materials that make sound.
- For this activity you'll need an even number of people (if you have one extra they can be a judge).
- Have enough containers for each person. Fill up containers in pairs with the same material until they are half full (so they make sound when you shake them). Here are some suggestions: water, sand, pebbles, loose mud (lots of water), small rocks, twigs, dried peas, acorns (if available), maple keys. Feel free to improvise, providing each pair makes a distinctive sound.
- Divide your group into two equal teams. Make sure each person has just one of the paired sound makers.
- Have the two teams stand about 15 feet (5 meters) apart in an area that is flat and clear (a park would do nicely).
- Ask participants to place their blindfolds on. On a given signal, have each group member begin shaking their sound maker and start walking slowly toward the other team. Remind participants to be careful so that they don't bump into one another. Can they find their match by sound alone?

Have participants try to guess what natural material makes their sound. Could they guess correctly? Ask participants to describe the sound each container made. What does this sound remind them of in the natural world? For example, the container of water might be reminiscent of a bubbling brook, the shaken pebbles may recall a rain storm, or perhaps the sound of sand conjures up the image of a sunny beach.

Sound makers

Credit: Jacob Rodenburg.

Group Wolf Howl

Many animals use sound as a way to locate others of their kind. A good example is the howl of a wolf. Amazingly, wolf howls can be heard as far away as 6 miles (9.6 kilometers). Wrapped up in this spine tingling and haunting vocalization are a number of possible messages. Wolves howl for some of the same reasons that people sing or cry out. They howl to let one another know of their location. They may howl as a warning signal to other packs saying: "stay clear of our territory." It might be used as a signal for the pack to meet up. Males might show their fitness and strength by howling to females (a lower more resonate tone indicates a larger, healthier wolf). Wolves often howl in packs—their voices harmonizing,

Wolf howl

Credit: Pixabay.

which can fool other wolves into thinking that there are more wolves present in the pack than there actually are.

Why not try out a realistic wolf howl for yourself? You'll need a group of eight or more participants.

- Select one participant with a strong voice to start you off. They are the Alpha Wolf (or the boss wolf) that often induces the pack to howl. Have them fill their lungs with air and let loose with a primal howl.
- Choose a Beta Wolf (the second in charge) to join in. Try harmonizing—or howling at slightly different pitches.
- Have half the group join in with

howls striving for different pitches (to sound like more wolves). Lastly have the rest of the group, as puppies, join in. They don't have fully developed vocal cords, so they sound more like Yip, Yowl, Yip, Yip, Yowl... Go on for a minute or so.

Feel better? There is nothing quite like howl therapy to help you vanquish the tensions of the day! And you've just created a realistic rendition of a pack wolf howl.

Visit YouTube and search wolf howls to see how your group howl compared to the howls of a real wolf pack.

NATURE MUSIC

The natural world is replete with all kinds of sound. And each material in nature has its own special quality of sound. Think about sticks clacking together or water sloshing in a bowl. What about the rustle of leaves or the crunch of snow underfoot?

- In this activity, have participants create a musical piece by gathering and using only natural sounds and arranging them in a sequence. For example, one person might rhythmically move their foot back and forth along a carpet of leaves, next another could tap sticks, while afterward another might clack stones together. The piece should have a beginning, middle, and end. Try layering different sounds on top of one another.

- Have participants practice this a few times before they share their creation with the group. Can they find a creative name for their nature musical piece? Perhaps a forest fugue, a meadow melody or a pine pizzicato.

Reading Nature's Music

Here is an activity for those that can read music and play an instrument.

You'll need two poles and enough string to create a musical staff (5 strings about 6 inches apart). About 8 feet (2.5 meters) wide should do the trick.

- Cut out a series of musical notes from card stock and tape clothes pins on the back of each one.
- Place the musical staff in front of a tree with low-hanging branches.

Wherever the branch crosses a staff line, place a musical note there.

- Using your musical instrument, read the notes and play this natural piece of music.
- Move the staff around to other places. Whenever you have a piece of music that really resonates with you, take a picture of the notes—and use these series of notes as a theme, to create an even longer musical piece.

Or try this:

- Use a blank piece of musical staff paper. Sit down outside and look at the horizon. Draw the curving lines of where the land and sky meet onto your staff paper.
- Everywhere your curving line intersects with the lines on the staff paper, place a musical note. You can select whatever type of note you like.
- Now play this musical piece, inspired by the sweep of the horizon—this is the land and sky singing to you.

Nature Music

Seasonal Sound Activities

- During the winter, listen to the noise of snow underfoot. The colder it gets, the squeakier snow sounds. You can really hear snow squeak and crunch below temperatures of 12°F (–11°C). This is due to delicate ice crystals that break and crack when we step on them. When it is warmer, the pressure from your foot causes the snow crystals to bend and melt.

- Notice how, after a fresh snow fall, sound is more muffled. Snow absorbs sound and after a winter storm there is a kind of soft silence that is both peaceful and soothing. If there is wind, tune into the music that creaking branches make.

- When it first starts to get cold, experiment with the sounds of ice. Gently tapping icicles together will make a distinctive and delicate tinkling. Listening to a lake freezing in winter creates a whole cacophony of sound from booms, moans, and crackles. There are thrumming noises reminiscent of the lasers used in *Star Wars* that you can hear when large expanses of ice begin to freeze.

- In autumn, listen to the crunching of leaves underfoot. How does the sound change from one part of the forest to the next?

- Listen for the squawks of blue jays, the calls of chickadees, but also notice the lack of bird song.

- In spring, tune into the amazing symphony of a melting stream—the gurgling, spluttering, and joyous sound of ice melting. When it rains, focus on the quality of sound rain makes as it spills over bushes and trees or even as it patters against your umbrella.

- Tune into the wonderful bird chorus at dawn and the joyful frog symphony in the evening.

- In summer, pay attention to the different sounds wind makes through trees, bushes, grasses, and over a lake. Focus on the sound of waves crashing against the shore. Close your eyes. Can you imagine the size and shape of each wave just by listening?

- Listen for the buzzing, chirruping, and clicking of the insect chorus.

SEEING NATURE

FOR MOST OF US, the world is a rich tapestry of color, shapes, and textures. We perceive up to 80% of the information about the world around us through our sense of sight. The eyes dominate our sensory experience.

For those who are vision impaired, there is research to suggest that the brain can rewire to allocate more space to regions in the brain responsible for processing other senses, such has hearing and smell.

Some anthropologists think that thousands of years ago our abstract thinking evolved as we tried to understand the complex visual environment surrounding us. Our ancestors used color as a way of determining whether fruit was ripe enough to eat and also to gain cues about whether a particular plant was poisonous. Today, in this fast-paced, technologically saturated world, we stare at colored screens as a way to interface with our environment. We spend more time on computers, smart phones, and TV monitors than almost any other pastime.

The idea of "seeing" is a metaphor deeply embedded in our language. When we understand, we say "I see." When we need proof, we might say "seeing is believing" or "go and see for yourself." We imagine our point of view or our perspective as belonging to our vision. As Marcel Proust put it: "The real voyage of discovery consists of not in seeking new landscapes, but in having new eyes." To have vision means to have a clear understanding of how one thinks the world ought to be. Vision is an integral part of our imagination. Our dreams are steeped in visual imagery. We make sense of the world by how we picture it.

OUR VISUAL SYSTEM

Take a look at a deer's eyes. Notice that they are on either side of her head? She has the eyes of an animal that is hunted. She is prey. Her eyes bulge outward, placed in this way to optimize her field of vision and primed to notice even the slightest of movements. You and I, on the other hand, have the eyes of a predator—just like a hawk. Our eyes are made to judge both distance and depth. We have stereoscopic vision that can hone in on an object and track accurately where it

is in space and time. But we need both eyes working together to have three-dimensional vision.

Try this. Hold out your hands straight in front of you with your index fingers pointed toward each other. Close one eye. Now slowly bring your fingers together and see if you can get them to touch each other. Now try with two eyes open. It's easier with two eyes, isn't it? That is because now you have gained depth perception, or the ability to tell

Eyes of deer

Credit: iStock.

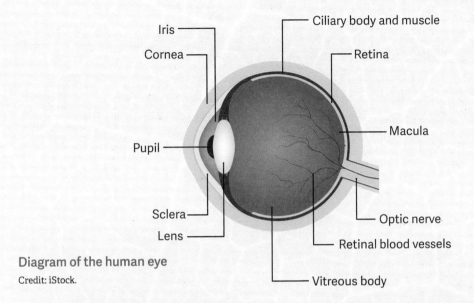

Iris

Cornea

Pupil

Sclera

Lens

Ciliary body and muscle

Retina

Macula

Optic nerve

Retinal blood vessels

Vitreous body

Diagram of the human eye
Credit: iStock.

how far away something is. Each eye gives slightly different information because of its angle to the object. Our brain processes this information and helps us judge distance. For a further challenge, try to touch the edges of two pennies together with your hands extended straight out in front of you—several times with one eye closed and compare this with two eyes open.

How our eyes see is nothing short of miraculous. Light is reflected into our eyes from an object (say a leaf). The light travels and enters the eyes through the cornea, a protective coating that stops dirt, germs, and other foreign objects from contaminating our eyes. The pupil (basically a hole) surrounded by the iris controls how much light goes into our eyes. Special ciliary muscles can adjust the shape of the lens to help us focus. Distant images cause the lens to thin,

closer objects cause the lens to thicken. The image of the leaf ends up in the back of our eye and is, incredibly, upside down. This is because the rays of light cross over onto the curved surface of the retina and onto an area packed with photoreceptors, known as rods and cones. Shaped like small gnome hats, three different types of cones (and there are over 6 million of them!) can each detect a different wavelength of the colors red, green, and blue. The blending of those colors yields the incredible palette of colors we see in the world around us. Rods (125 million of them) are designed to help us with night vision. They are sensitive to light but cannot detect color. The image of the leaf is then sent via nerve impulses along the optic nerve, from the photoreceptors up to our brain. Our brain interprets this and flips the image right side up again. How cool is that!

SEASONAL COLORS

Each season has its signature colour palette. Summer is the time of crimson, blues, whites, and yellows. During autumn, the hues of gold, yellow, red, and orange draw thousands of people to the Northeast to bear witness to the dramatic color change in leaves. Winter is characterized by shades of white, grey, dark green (conifers), tan, and brown.

Credit: Pixabay and designed by David Lindblad.

Spring seasonal color wheel

It is tempting to want to blend everything together into one color. That forest may just look like a smear of green. But hold a leaf or a blade of grass next to a color chip and you really become aware of how many shades there are. Here is an activity to help you appreciate the tremendous variety of color in the natural world.

- Color photocopy the seasonal color wheels provided in this book.
- Provide each participant with a small bag of clothes pins.

Summer seasonal color wheel

• Can participants find something in nature that precisely matches the colors on this wheel? There are photos of actual objects in nature along with their corresponding color. How close does your natural object match the corresponding inner color? If you find a match, clip a small piece of the object with the cloths pin, onto this spot to show that you found it.

Fall seasonal color wheel

- Try this activity throughout each season of the year.
- You can also obtain paint chips from your nearby paint store. How many of these

shades are found in nature? What are seasonal colors are you finding?

Winter seasonal color wheel

Pirate eye

Do we really see the colors we think we see?

- Find a quiet spot where there are lots of colors.
- Shut one eye and cover it with your hand. Leave your hand there for at least three minutes. Observe your spot through your one open eye.
- After about three minutes, switch between your eyes, opening one eye, then the other. Do this repeatedly. What do you notice? The shades of colors have completely changed between your eyes! That is because one pupil (the black spot in the middle of your eyes) dilated—got bigger—when you closed it. When you open your eyes again, the world looks brighter through this eye. The other eye, with a smaller pupil, creates darker shades. So which eye reveals the true colors of the world around us?
- Do you think all humans see exactly in the same shades? We humans can distinguish between two to three million shades of color. Many insects, like bees, can see beyond the visible spectrum and detect ultraviolet light. To bees, flowers have totally different-looking patterns and colors. For example, the ultraviolet light often reveals stripes on the petals which guide hungry bees to the nectar.

Pirate eye

Credit: Jacob Rodenburg.

CAMOUFLAGED ANIMALS/COUNTERSHADING

Nearby where I work is a lovely natural area. There is nothing I like better than exploring. And sometimes, I leave the trails to go and find places that I've never been to before. It was during one of these forays into the woods that I heard a tremendous whirling of feathers. A ruffed grouse exploded into the air right next to my foot. She then began to do her broken wing trick, dragging one of her wings along the ground to make it seem like she was hurt. I then recalled that she does this to lead predators away from her nest. And sure enough, when I looked down, I spotted her leafy nest nearby on the forest floor with twelve speckled cream eggs nestled inside. I hadn't seen the grouse nor her eggs because she was so beautifully camouflaged. She had remained completely still until I ventured too close. Being frozen in place, meant that her brown, black, and tan coloring helped her to vanish into the landscape. But when she felt it was too dangerous, she burst upward from the forest floor, giving her just enough time to deflect my attention away from the eggs.

Many animals use camouflage as a way to protect themselves. The use of color and patterning to help an animal hide is called concealment camouflage. Hiding works best when you are completely still. That is why you'll notice an animal frequently stops and freezes—then moves again when it is safe.

There are so many examples of camouflage in nature, from the mottled green color of frogs to the rusty brown pattern on the wings of a moth. Animals also use countershading as a further way to protect themselves. This means they are slightly lighter from underneath. Look at the belly of a frog or a white-tailed deer, and it is noticeably paler. When light falls on a three-dimensional object, it naturally appears lighter on top and darker on the bottom. Countershading helps offset this by doing just the opposite and helping to break the form and shape of the animal. There is also mimicry—a walking stick insect is a great example of this. Animals take on the form and shape of something else to conceal their true selves. From imitating bird

Ruffed grouse

Credit: Pixabay.

poop to mimicking predators' eyes (when polyphemus moths flash their hind wings, they reveal an oval shape reminiscent of an owl's eyes), there are literally thousands of ways insects, birds, and mammals imitate other things in order to hide and deceive. Their survival depends on a convincing disguise!

Camouflage Animal Game

- Photocopy the colored animals on pages 43–45. Laminate these if you can.

- Go to a nearby greenspace: a park, schoolyard, or backyard.
- Provide one animal per pair of participants. Establish boundaries.

Camouflaged animals

Credit: all Pixabay.

- Have one participant close their eyes (the seeker) while another (the hider) selects a spot to hide their animal. Ask the hider to really think about where their animal might best be camouflaged. Perhaps the rabbit can be tucked under a bush or the toad can be laid against some leaves or dried grass.
- Have the seeker try to find the animal within a given space of time. Switch roles (the hider becomes the seeker and vice versa). If there is time, switch animals.

CAMOUFLAGED EGGS

If you think about it, a bird egg is a beautiful thing. Within this fragile container comes the promise of new feathered life. And bird eggs come in a surprising variety of shapes, sizes, and colors. But no matter what they look like there is one fact that may seem obvious but deserves mention—eggs roll. And a rolling egg is not a safe egg. Keeping their eggs both warm and safe is the challenge every mother bird faces. That is why she makes a nest. Sometimes it is an elaborate affair like the woven hanging nest of a northern oriole, or sometimes it is as simple as a hollow scrape in the ground like that of a killdeer. Birds that lay their eggs on cliffs, like common murres, often have pointy eggs. That way if an egg rolls, it will roll in a tight circle instead of falling off the cliff face.

Killdeer eggs

Credit: iStock.

Many ground-nesting birds rely on camouflaged eggs to protect them. Often, they will mimic the microhabitat they are in. For example, the mottled, striped, and spotted pattern of a killdeer egg can mimic the surrounding vegetation and rocks. There are two main egg pigments that create the amazing diversity of color and pattern in eggs. The reddish-brown color comes from the pigment called protoporphyrin, and the pigment biliverdin creates the hues of blue and green. By regulating how much of each pigment is laid down, each mother bird creates the unique and varied background colors and markings that are characteristic of her eggs.

Make Your Own Camouflaged Egg

- You'll need hard-boiled brown chicken eggs (one for each participant), markers, and/or acrylic paints.
- Check out the photos of bird eggs on the internet. Study their patterns and colors. Have each participant color an egg, using these pictures as a guide.
- Just like the camouflaged egg activity, have one person close their eyes and the other hide their egg. Select an area that best matches the color pattern you've created.
- Now switch. If you like, peel and eat your eggs, being careful not to get any coloring on the edible part of the egg.

Homemade camouflaged egg

Credit: Jacob Rodenburg.

NATURE SCULPTING

There is art in nature everywhere. Andy Goldsworthy knows this. He is a remarkable artist who uses natural materials to create inspiring art. He might pin up colored leaves in the fall using thorns and allow the light to shine through. Or he might create beautiful spherical objects using intertwining branches. He even breathes icicles together to create a frozen star. Goldsworthy uses material he finds in nature, and he makes art with his hands only; he doesn't use tools of any kind. He then takes a picture and allows the natural world to reclaim his creation.

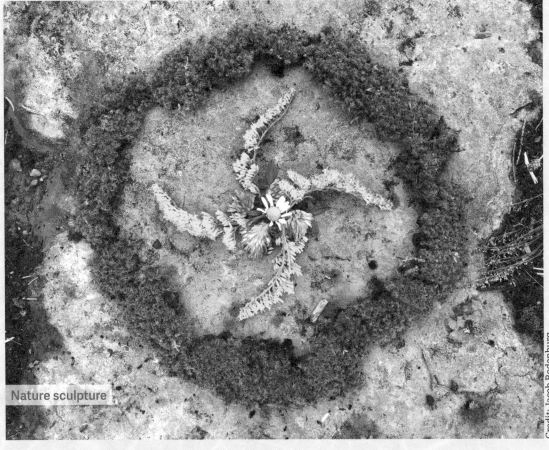

Nature sculpture

Credit: Jacob Rodenburg.

Nature Sculpture

You too can make a beautiful nature sculpture. Here is how:

- Find a natural area that is not too heavily impacted by humans.
- If you can, take a look at Andy Goldsworthy's art for some ideas. You'll find plenty of examples on the internet.
- It is important to discuss responsible harvesting. If you are going to pick something—say a wildflower or small section of an evergreen bough—only take a little bit from one area and then move along. Never pick a whole plant. Or you can simply say only make your sculpture out of dead material.
- Practice reciprocity. I often take seeds with me and plant them as a way of giving back to the environment.
- In groups of two or three, create a nature sculpture—think about pattern, color, form, texture, shape. It can be flat on the ground, freestanding, or hanging from something.
- Have participants name their creation.
- Take a photo of each piece.
- It is time for an art exhibit. Go for a tour of the various sculptures. Take along a small glass of grape juice (or older people can use wine) and savor the natural forms.
- Allow the natural world to reconstitute the art into something natural once again. Share with others.

Framing Nature

Sometimes, just by isolating a small piece of the natural world, you'll see it in an entirely different way. Try an old photographer's trick.

- Take one hand and extend it outward. Turn your hand inward with your thumb pointing down and your fingers pressed together. Extend your other hand and flip your hand with your thumb pointing upward. Joint your two hands together, and you should have a frame that you can see through.
- Close one eye and scan the natural world for an image that really captivates you.

- Visit an area that has the potential for some eye-catching views. It could be where the edge of a lawn meets the woods, or perhaps a curving hill or a meandering pathway.
- Take with you some rope, twine, or string, some empty frames, and some clothes pins. To make an empty frame, you could simply take a cardboard box and, using a utility knife and a ruler, cut out the fame with a 1-inch border a 12 × 12 inch (25 cm) frame seems to work nicely. Or go to your local paint store and ask for wooden paint stirrers. Simply glue or nail four of these together into a square—now you have reusable frames.
- Tie your rope, string, or twine about eye level across various points that look appealing.
- Ask your participants to hang their frames using two clothes pins, anywhere along the rope that looks appealing to them. When they've selected their perfect spot, ask them to provide a name for their piece.
- You can also simply pin your frame on a tree branch, or lay your frame on the ground. Or hold your frame skyward so you can frame clouds.
- Have an art exhibit where you all have an opportunity to see each other's creation.

Framing Nature

Credit: Jacob Rodenburg.

Japanese Viewing Party

How wonderful the unfurling of the petals of a flower! In Japan, people practice *Hanami*, or flower-viewing. They sip plum brandy and sit and watch as cherry blossoms emerge, petal by petal, on a warm spring day. The concept of watching something beautiful in nature, for example, a sunset or a sunrise, with intention and in community, can be a powerful experience.

Create your own viewing party:

- Find something lovely in nature. It doesn't have to be big to be beautiful. Perhaps a small grove of wildflowers, an interestingly shaped tree, some moss-covered rocks, or a small stream.
- Ask your participants to silently walk with you. Arrange yourselves so that everyone has a nice view. Simply sit still and watch.
- If you'd like, hand out plum brandy or orange juice in small glasses. Sip and quietly soak in the beauty that is around you. Give it the time that it requires. Don't be in a rush. Silently watching as the natural world unfolds of its own accord is a wonderful counterpoint to the frenzy of our fast-paced modern world.
- Offer up your time, your mindfulness, and your patience to truly savor that which you are immersed in. You will feel a sense of belonging and connectedness that all of us yearn for. And in so doing, you will feel that much more complete.

Japanese viewing party

Credit: iStock.

Etched in My Hand—a Branch

In the book *The Geography of Childhood*, authors Gary Paul Naban and Stephen Trimble ask us to "look into every face." What they mean by this is that often we are in a hurry to see things at a species level. We see an oak tree, we notice a chickadee, and we spot yet another grey squirrel gallivanting in the park. Yet, we tend to forget that each living thing is an individual too. That particular elm, with its branches arching outward and a large hole halfway up its trunk, the way it towers over a clump of rock and has a lightening scar just above where the main trunk forks—that elm has only occurred once on this Earth, nor will it ever come again. It is lovely and it is unique. Just like you. And just like every other living thing in nature.

- To help your participants appreciate individuality, select a large tree that has space to lie down underneath.
- Ask everyone to lie backward, forming a circle with heads together and feet

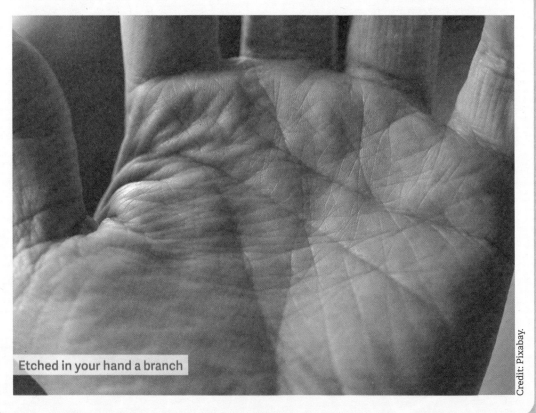

Etched in your hand a branch

Credit: Pixabay.

pointing outward. Have them stare up into the canopy of the tree.

- Ask them to examine the bottom wrinkles of their open hand. Those who study palms call these the life line and the head line. Notice how they look a lot like branches of a tree?

- Can your participants find a branching pattern that exactly matches these lines on their palms?

- Gather together and ask everyone to point out their branch. There, that is their branch—as unique and exceptional as they are.

Poetree

- Ask participants to think about a tree or a living thing that they've had a special relationship with while growing up.
- To further honor their connection to this tree, encourage them to think about one stanza of poetry that reflects this experience. Tell them this is known as Poetree.
- Combine your stanzas of Poetree and share.

You might try a Japanese haiku. These brief poems consist of five syllables in the first line, seven in the second, and five syllables in the third. Their very brevity makes them evocative. What kinds of haikus can you come up with? Here is one:

Your deep inhaling
Gathers in sweet oxygen
Gifted from this tree

Here is one of mine.

The sweep of this branch
Is the joining of green, blue, and brown
The sweet touch of sun and sky and earth
Imagine a green-fingered hand stretching
    above
Gathering life to all that is below

HAIKU

Basement Windows

Much of what goes on in the world is hidden from view. There is a magical underworld replete with tiny dragons, earth-boring submarines, and shape shifters. All you need to do is peek! To discover these special places, simply venture into a forest. Before you go, provide each person with a magnifying glass if possible and a small container (glass jar, yogurt container, or bug jar).

• Ask your participants to carefully lift up a rock or a log and look underneath. These are the windows into the world below. You might be lucky enough to spot a salamander (looks a bit like a very small dragon) or a plump earthworm (these have the capability of plunging down deep just like a submarine). You might even see a pill bug, a tiny crustacean that rolls up into a tight ball when threatened (a shape-shifter). What magical

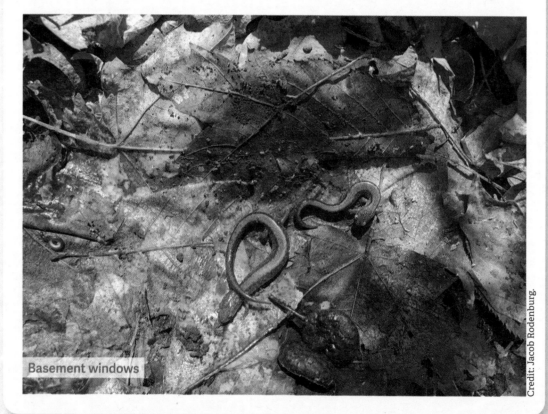

Basement windows

creatures can you find? What are they and how do they help to maintain a healthy and diverse forest ecosystem?

- Can you spot the "wood wide web?" Look for tiny threads, minuscule filaments of a fungal organism that wrap themselves in and around tree roots. This "*mycorrhizal network*" helps to transfer water, nitrogen, carbon and other minerals between trees. In this way trees can "talk" to each other through these fungal networks.

- Earthworms help to aerate the soil and provide nutrients with their castings (worm poo). Thousands of fungi, bacteria, millipedes, and pill bugs decompose leaves, branches, and wood, helping to create rich and fertile soil. Many beetles and their larvae are an important food source for mammals, amphibians, and birds.

- If you can, have everyone carefully scoop their critter discoveries into a container.

- Have each participant sit in a circle facing inward. On a given signal, have everyone pass their container to the right at the same time. Ask one of the questions posed below then pass your critter again to the right. Continue this pattern. Here are some sample questions. Feel free to ask your own.

- How does your critter move?
- Can you see it breathing?
- Insects have compound eyes (or many little eyes bunched into one eye). Can you see your critter's eyes?
- Examine your critter's mouth parts. What do you think it eats? Does it have chomping parts (like a grasshopper), sucking parts (like a mosquito), sponge parts (like a housefly) or biting parts (like a deerfly)?
- How many body segments does your critter have? A true insect has a head, a thorax (middle part), and an abdomen (stomach). A spider only has two body parts and therefore is not an insect (it is an arachnid).
- Is your critter camouflaged? Think about where you found it.
- How might your critter protect itself?
- What do you think your critter is? If you can, have an insect field guide handy as a resource.

Please place back your critters exactly where you found them. Don't forget to gently close your window, being careful not to squish or harm your discovery.

Night Hike

To Know the Dark

To go in the dark with a light is to know the light.
To know the dark, go dark. Go without sight,
and find that the dark, too, blooms and sings,
and is traveled by dark feet and dark wings.

Terrapin And Other Poems by Wendell Berry

There is something magical about the experience of being in nature at night. Take a night hike, but as Wendell Berry suggests, leave the flashlight off and go "dark."

- Choose a well-defined trail in an area that you know well, away from city lights. This is a great opportunity to activate your other senses as well as your sight. The musty smell of damp earth underfoot, the gentle chirruping of crickets, the feeling of cool night air brushed against your cheek, and most special of all, the sparkling canopy of stars overhead.

- At the end of your hike, close one eye and keep it closed. Strike a match and stare at this for 10 or more seconds with your open eye (keep the other shut). Now blow out the match. Open

Night hike

Credit: iStock.

one eye at a time and notice the difference in your night vision.

- The eye that was closed retains its night vision, while the one that was staring at the lit match, lost its night vision. You'll notice an incredible difference in how much more you can see through the dark adjusted eye. This is because our eyes contain rhodopsin, a chemical that is highly sensitive to light. Rhodopsin quickly breaks down, so it takes a while for our eyes to regenerate this chemical. It can take up to 2 hours for our eyes to become fully adjusted to seeing in the dark, but you can gain some night vision in as little as 15 minutes.

Tree Faces

The human brain is very good at seeing "faces," even when they are not really there. Next time you go for a walk in the woods, scan for tree faces. They might consist of two knots for eyes and a small cavity for a mouth. Mark your find with a small ribbon. Do other people see what you see? Old willows have a lot of gnarly, twisted trunks that make them an ideal tree to look for faces.

You may also see faces in rock formations or in patterns of plants on the forest floor. Take a picture and share.

Tree faces

Credit: Pixabay.

Mirror Walk

Are you a foot watcher? Do you walk with your eyes cast down? When we adjust our perspective, we see the world in new and refreshing ways. That is what a mirror walk will allow you to do. Purchase some inexpensive mirrors. Hand one out to each person (or share if there aren't enough). Encourage participants to view the "underworld" by holding a mirror on the underside of a leaf or a flower. You can also walk along a trail and view the canopy of trees from your mirror.

Splatter Vision

When we walk in a natural setting, we tend to focus our eyes in front of us. This makes sense because we want to know if there are any hazards that we might trip over. However, by focusing only what is ahead, we miss what is going on behind, above and to the sides of us. Practice being an "all around watcher" and use what naturalists call "splatter vision." This means not keeping your eyes in one place for too long. Try to get in the habit of looking in all directions and distances. For example, occasionally look ahead of where you are walking, such as a good distance down the road or path; scan the sky from time to time; when you arrive at a body of water, look for any dark objects (e.g., possible ducks, loons, beaver) swimming or floating on the surface; check out the crowns of trees, dead branches, and telephone wires for birds; be as aware as possible, too, of your peripheral vision. This helps you tune into movement at the edges of your field of vision. You can practice extending your peripheral vision by looking straight forward but placing your fingers on either side of your head. Waggle your index fingers and slowly move both of your fingers back until you can't see them anymore. Keep practicing and you can extend your field of vision. Some of your most amazing discoveries can be out of the corner of your eye.

Splatter vision

Credit: Jacob Rodenburg.

Micro-trails

Einstein once said: "Imagination is more important than knowledge. Imagination is the language of the soul. Pay attention to your imagination and you will discover all you need to be fulfilled." With your imagination, you can gain a whole new appreciation for the natural world. So, using the power of your imagination, shrink yourself down to the size of an ant. What would the forest look like if you were only a fraction of an inch tall? What points of interest might capture your attention? Perhaps a funny-colored mushroom, a chewed leaf, or an interesting groove on a fallen log? Try this:

- Get 10 to 20 Popsicle sticks and about 30 feet (10 meters) of colorful yarn or string. Using these simple materials, create a micro-trail. Find at least eight points of interest no more than a few steps from each other. You might find an interesting hole in the ground, a spider's web, or an animal track.
- Beside each point of interest, press a Popsicle stick into the ground. Connect all the points with the twine by wrapping it a couple of times around each stick and extending the string to your next Popsicle stick until all points are joined in one long line. This becomes your micro-trail.

- When you are finished, sit down and quietly watch the trail for a few minutes. Then, get down on your hands and knees and take a trip along the trail, keeping your head close to the ground. Better still, use a magnifying glass or a hand lens and really study things up close. Take someone special to your micro-trail and give them a guided tour of your discoveries!

Micro-trails

Credit: Jacob Rodenburg.

Eagle Eyes

Just how keen are your eyes compared to an eagle? Here is a simple way to find out.

- Tie a bright colored piece of thread or yarn around a post or tree. Now walk backward. Stop when you no longer can see the thread.
- How far can go before you no longer can see it? An eagle can resolve this up to 10 times further than you can. In other words, if you could just barely see the thread at 150 feet (50 meters), an eagle can spot that same thread from 1500 feet (500 meters) away!

Human Camera

This activity works well in groups of 10 to 30. But you can also do this with just 2 participants. You'll need pieces of paper about the same size as a standard photo and assorted colored pencils or markers.

- Divide the group into pairs. Ask one of the pair to close their eyes. The other person (the guide) carefully steers them to a beautiful or an interesting spot in nature, while their eyes remain closed. It might be an up-close view of a flower; or perhaps a curiously twisting tree branch. It could even be a lovely vista.
- Carefully sit the participant down, eyes still shut. They have become a human camera. To operate the shutter, the guide lightly taps their head. Or you can gently tug on an earlobe if you feel comfortable doing so. The participant is instructed to open

Human camera

Credit: Jacob Rodenburg.

their eyes just for a few seconds. Ask them to focus (ha!) and to take a clear mental picture of what it is in front of them. Then ask them to close their eyes again while they are guided back.

- When you've returned, have the participant develop their print. This means that using the colored pencils/ markers provided, they'll draw, as accurately as they can, the photo that they had just taken a mental picture of. Make sure that the guide does not see the developed picture.

- Now switch roles so that the guide is the human camera. Make sure a second picture is developed. When each pair have had a chance to take and develop pictures, assemble them all on a table for a photo exhibit. Can the guides identify the scene that they took their participant to?

This is a wonderful activity for heightening awareness of the beauty, texture, pattern, color, and composition of scenes within the natural world.

Clothes Pin View

We forget how nature can change so rapidly. When we go for a walk, we tend to notice what is right in front of us. To truly appreciate how quickly the natural world changes over time, try this:

- During the spring or fall, take a clothes pin and write your name on it. Clip it to a tree bud during spring or to a green leaf during late summer, just as the trees are about to change color. Visit your clothes pin each day and notice how your bud or leaf transforms. If you can, take a photograph of your bud or leaf every day. By focusing on one particular spot in the natural world, we begin to appreciate the beauty, yet ephemeral nature of life.

Clothes pin view

Credit: Jacob Rodenburg.

Deer Walking

If you can, take the time to really observe a robin as she moves along the ground. Notice how she stops, looks around, hops a few steps, quickly pecks for food, stares, and then hops again. Many animals use this method as a way to move through the landscape, not only to forage for food but also to stop and pay attention to their surroundings. When we humans walk through the environment, we tend to plod along at a consistent speed. Many predatory animals move in this same way. A fox, a wolf, or a coyote have what is known as a harmonic gate—a purposeful walk that helps them move quickly and efficiently from one spot to another so that they can cover their hunting territory.

We can learn from animals that need to be wary of their surroundings. A deer's ears are constantly swivelling; their nose is twitching; their bulging eyes, positioned on either side of their head, help them to take in a wide swath of the landscape. Their survival depends on them being utterly alert. At the same time, they often stop and stand stock-still—this allows them to take in their surroundings. When they stand perfectly still, their fur helps them to blend into the forest. In this simple activity, we will mimic these movements so that, just like deer, we can be more aware of the natural world around us.

- Pick a number in your head. Say 5. Now take 5 steps and freeze for 5 seconds. While frozen, try to activate your sense of sight, hearing, and smell.
- Pick another number. Say 10. Take 10 steps and freeze for 10 seconds.
- Keep up this pattern of selecting a number and taking this number of steps and freezing for that length of time.
- Compare this to a regular walk. Did you notice a difference? Were you more aware of the natural world around you?

SHAPES IN NATURE

Nature is full of complex curves, shapes, and lines. To our eyes, the natural world seems messy—a confusing array of colours, forms, texture, and objectives. But a more careful look reveals how intricate and beautiful the shapes of nature can be.

Shape Scavenger Hunt

This activity helps us to see just how varied the forms of nature can be. Copy the Nature Shape Bingo Scavenger Hunt card provided on the next page. Take a walk through a nearby natural area. How many shapes can you find?

Nature shape bingo scavenger hunt

Credit: Pixabay.

NATURE SHAPE BINGO CARD (CAN YOU FIND...) FILL IN A ROW, COLUMN OR DIAGONAL FOR A BINGO

	B	**I**	**N**	**G**	**O**
B	HEART SHAPE	TRIANGLE SHAPE	ROUND SHAPE	OVAL SHAPE	STAR SHAPE
I	RECTANGLE SHAPE	CURVE SHAPE	BILATERAL SYMETRY (ONE SIDE IS A REFLECTION OF THE OTHER SIDE)	RADIAL SYMETRY (ROTATE THE SHAPE AND IT LOOKS THE SAME)	A SPIRAL SHAPE
N	LEAF WITH WAVY EDGES	LEAF WITH POINTED EDGES	ELLIPTIC LEAF (LONG, NARROW AND POINTED)	SERRATED LEAF (TOOTHED EDGE)	RENIFORM LEAF (KIDNEY SHAPED)
G	LEAF WITH PALMATE VEINING (VEINS SPREAD FROM CENTRAL POINT)	LEAF WITH PINNATE VEINING (VEINS RUN NEXT TO EACH OTHER)	LEAF WITH ARCUATE VEINING (VEINS BEND TO A POINT)	AN ACICULAR LEAF (NEEDLE SHAPED)	FRACTAL (BRANCHING PATTERN)
O	HEXAGON SHAPE	SOMETHING IN NATURE WITH A STRAIGHT EDGE	SOMETHING CYLINDRICAL	MOUNDED SHAPE	YOUR OWN SHAPE DISCOVERY

The Book of Nature Connection Worksheets are available for free download at:
https://newsociety.com/pages/book-of-nature-connection-worksheets

Wind-wanderers

If you think about it, plants can't move. And yet, each year new plants grow, often far away from the parent plant. How does this happen? Over time, plants have developed ingenious ways of dispersing their seeds. Some stick, some are pooped out, and some dance on the wind. Consider the delicate plume of a dandelion seed, the twirling maple key, and even a tiny-winged pine seed that falls out of a pinecone. These seeds ride the wind currents until they land on a patch of soil and a new plant takes root.

In this activity, use an egg carton to collect these wind-wanderers. Keep the lid closed as you travel to the next spot looking for bits of nature that can become airborne. It doesn't have to be a seed. Perhaps you'll find a curiously shaped leaf that reminds you of a sail, or a blade of grass that can ride on the wind. Study how each wind-wanderer moves. Run your fingers along the shape of your bit of nature to feel the parts that help it to float.

Gather as a group. Release your wind-wanderer. Can you imitate its movement with your own body to create a wind dance? You might float gently, spin and weave, or flutter. Work together to create a performance that incorporates all of your movements.

Fibonacci Sequence

Mathematics has never been my strong point. But there is something beautiful and harmonious about the regular patterning found in nature—from the spiral of a snail's shell to the colorful arrangements of petals on a flower; from the position of scales on a pinecone to the way that leaves clasp onto a stem. And what is wonderful is that these patterns and so many others in the natural world follow a particular mathematical rule called the Fibonacci sequence. Although known by Indian mathematicians for centuries, the sequence was made popular to the rest of the world by an Italian merchant named Leonardo de Pisa over 800 years ago. It is both elegant and powerful. The sequence is: 1, 1, 2, 3, 5, 8, 13, 21, 34, 55, 89 . . .—each number is the sum of the previous two: $1 + 0 = 1, 1 + 2 = 3, 3 + 5 = 8, 8 + 5 = 13$ and so on. If you express this in terms of area, you begin to generate a spiral (see image on the following page).

Here's a few of the many things in nature that follow this rule:

- spiral of a snail's shell
- arrangement of seeds in a sunflower
- curling ferns
- petals on a flower
- scales on a pine cone

- our spiral galaxy
- folds of our ears
- shape of eggs
- ridges of our thumbprints
- patterns of clouds in a hurricane

Can you find other examples?

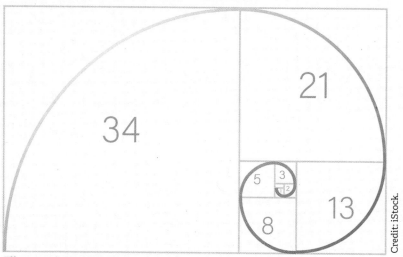

Fibonacci sequence

Credit: iStock.

Curiosity—Holmsing the Leaf

My colleague Paul Elliott once attended a workshop on beetles. He was taken by an interesting activity inspired by Sir Author Conan Doyle, the author of Sherlock Holmes. The workshop host spoke about how Dr. Watson was contin-

ually mystified by Holmes's keen powers of deduction. When asked by Watson about his remarkable abilities, Holmes simply replied, "My dear Watson, you see but you do not observe."

When we observe, we wonder. And

when we wonder, we begin to foster curiosity. And curiosity, if you think about it, is the engine of learning. When you're curious, you ask questions, you want to find out more. Here is an activity that helps to hone this skill. This works in groups of 2 or larger.

- Find a fallen leaf.
- Encourage each person to examine their leaf closely. Begin by having participants finish the statement: "I observe that…." For example:
  - I observe that the leaf is curved at the end.
  - I observe the veins are more pronounced on one side and less on the other.
  - I observe that the edges of my leaf are toothed.
  - I observe that there are different colors throughout my leaf.
- Make sure each participant has an opportunity to fully observe their leaf.
- Now have each person finish the following sentence: "I wonder…." For example:
  - I wonder why my leaf is the color green.
  - I wonder why the stem is flattened.
  - I wonder what made these small holes on my leaf.
  - I wonder what kind of plant this leaf came from.

- Lastly, have participants finish the following statement: "This leaf reminds me of…." For example:
  - This leaf reminds me of how varied leaves can be.
  - This leaf reminds me of autumn and the coming winter.
  - This leaf reminds me that plants get their food from leaves.
  - This leaf reminds me of how falling leaves nourish the soil and make it more fertile.

This activity moves from honing observation skills to asking wonder questions to building connections. Remember for every wonder question there is an answer, and every connection made helps to remind us just how marvellously interdependent the natural world really is.

Holmsing a leaf

Credit: Pixabay.

SEASONAL SIGHT ACTIVITIES

- In winter, try to guess the type of tree by its silhouette. Many species of conifers have their own unique shape.
- Take a picture during winter of a beautiful scene. Take a picture again from the same place throughout each season of the year. Note how the color palette for each season changes so dramatically.
- In spring, try to count how many distinctive shades of green you can discover. Use the Seasonal Color Wheel to help you (page 38).
- In fall, create a leaf rainbow by finding various shades and placing them next to each other, always going from lighter shades to darker. Move from green to yellow, from yellow to orange, from orange to red, from red to purple, from purple to tan, and from tan to brown.
- In summer, create a leaf collage. Find different colors of leaves. Use thorns or small twigs to pin them together so they are hanging. On a sunny day, watch how the light creates a stained glass effect, illuminating each leaf.

THE WORLD OF SMELL

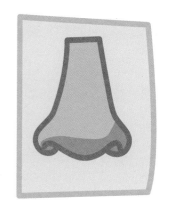

Aꜰ ᴛʜᴇ ꜱᴍᴇʟʟ of freshly baked apple pie! Perhaps you can remember eating pie and ice cream under the shade of an old oak tree with your aunt and uncle. Or maybe this smell conjures up images of Thanksgiving dessert. Of all the senses, our sense of smell is the one most directly connected to emotion and recall. That is because there is a pipeline straight from our nose to the region of the brain responsible for processing our feelings and our memories. And with every breath in and every breath out (about 23,000 times per day), we smell the world around us. We are awash in odors of all kinds, from the pleasant fragrance of lily to the sharp and pungent smell of fire. The latest research suggests that our sense of smell is far more sensitive that we give it credit for. If a friend is happy, they release subtle odors that make us happy, or if they are stressed or upset, we pick that up too, unconsciously of course. A 2014 study revealed that we detect up to 1 trillion distinct odors. And yet our vocabulary is limited when describing smells. We use words like floral, musky, minty, acrid, and rancid…but this barely begins to capture the rich and fragrant world that swirls around us.

It may be hard to believe, but some anthropologists theorize that it is our sense of smell that gave rise to our brain. Millions of years ago, a small clump of olfactory tissue developed rudimentary stalks. Gradually, as we used odor to sense the world around us, these buds of tissue became more and more complex, evolving into the two hemispheres of our brains. Perhaps one could say (to paraphrase Descartes) we smell, therefore we think.

OUR OLFACTORY SYSTEM

Take a deep breath through your nose. Notice how quickly air travels up your nasal cavities. What happens next? Molecules carrying odor make their way up high inside our nose to our olfactory bulb which contains dense sensory cells called olfactory sensory neurons. Each of these neurons has a single odor receptor. Odors may also travel from the roof of our mouth through a channel that connects directly to our nose. Chewing food such as chocolate cake releases aromas that connect to the same olfactory sensory neurons. Our sense of taste and smell are intimately connected. Whether it is the sweet smell of a rose or the taste of freshly baked bread, the sensory neurons transfer this information to our amygdala, a region in our brain that helps us recognize the odor. There are always more smells surrounding us than we can identify. And molecules can stimulate more than one receptor, creating a unique combination of odors we interpret as a particular smell.

Around the moist surface of your mouth, throat, nose, and eyes are many nerve endings that help you detect substances that are irritating, for example, the surprising coolness of menthol or the tearing effect of a pealed onion.

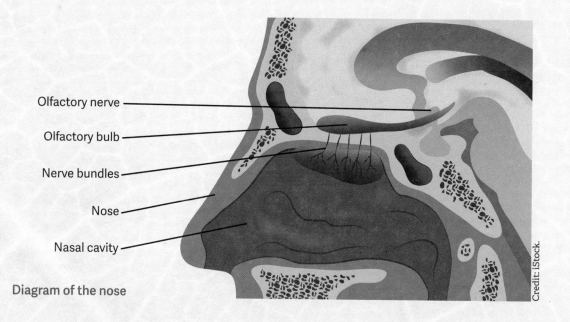

Olfactory nerve

Olfactory bulb

Nerve bundles

Nose

Nasal cavity

Diagram of the nose

Credit: iStock.

Scratch and Sniff

- Next time you go for a walk, take along some water and small pieces of sponge. Dab a moistened sponge under everyone's nose; just a little moisture on the upper lip will suffice. The wetness under your nose helps you to distinguish more odors.
- Now try a little "scratch and sniff." Gently rub the leaves of different trees and shrubs between your fingers. As you walk, rub moss and sniff. Gently caress some lichen and sniff.
- Take a small pinch of soil from a few different parts of the forest or field—do they smell different? Some farmers can gauge the fertility of the soil by its smell. Continue to caress and smell various parts of the natural world including leaves, bark, and twigs. The idea is to be gentle—you don't need to rub much to release an odor. If you have small children with you, make sure they rub what you rub just to ensure that they are not touching something that may be hazardous (poison ivy, giant hogweed, etc.).

Smell Cocktail

Now that you've practiced sniffing, you are ready for a cocktail party! A chance to mingle with friends and to sample something fragrant and soothing. Why not create your very own smell cocktail?

- You'll need a few paper cups and a small twig as a swizzle stick.
- As you hike, encourage participants to selectively harvest tiny bits of the forest (e.g., a pinch of soil, a part of a leaf, a petal of wildflower, a bud, a smidgen of moss, or a flake of bark). Always talk about mindful harvesting (taking just a tiny bit from here and a bit

Smell cocktail

Credit: Jacob Rodenburg.

from there and being careful not to cause too much damage in one spot). And if you can, practice reciprocity by planting some seeds. I often take along native wildflower seeds that I'll sprinkle near wherever we have been harvesting.

- Place each bit of nature in your cup. Add your swivel stick. Use the swizzle stick to gently crush the material inside your cup. This will help release the odors. You now have created your very own smell cocktail.
- Give each smell cocktail creation a name, perhaps "Pinesappyness" or "Woodilicious." Take time to smell each other's creations. Can you identify the fragrances?

Scent Trails

Imagine this. Your eyes are closed and you hunker down. You fill your lungs full of fresh spring air, and you pick up a scent. It is the familiar odor of your friend Rick, and you can tell that he passed right by your front door and is headed for downtown. You use your nose and you follow his scent right to a convenience store just in time to share his bag of chips. If only that were true!

Unfortunately, our human nose isn't sensitive enough to follow scent trails. But many animals can. Canids (or members of the dog family), including foxes, coyotes, wolves, and dogs, have an incredible sense of smell—many thousands of times better than a human. A larger portion of their brain is given over to scent perception. They can distinguish between many different types of smell. We might say, "hmmm mac and cheese." They might say, "hmmm noodles and cheese and butter and salt and milk and bread crumbs and metal pot and Aunt Marge must have just made this." Animals take short and deep sniffs to isolate and follow a scent.

In this game you'll be given a "helping nose" so that you can follow a scent trail to something delicious. Work in partners.

- One person is blindfolded while the other lays down a scent trail with extract. You can use simulated extract. Try lemon, almond, mint, maple, and orange extract. You only need a drop or two every foot or so for about five feet (1.5 meters). Try to lay down a curving, sweeping trail to make things more challenging.

- At the end of the scent trail, place a wrapped mint. Guide the blindfolded partner to the beginning of your trail and let them use their nose to follow the trail. And if you are lucky, just like a hunting fox following the trail of a rabbit, there might be something tasty at the end of your journey!

Scent Pouches

Ever notice how conifer (cone bearing) trees have a different smell? Whether it is pine, cedar, spruce, fir, or hemlock, each species has its own signature scent. Conifers produce terpenes, a chemical compound that protects them from insect and fungal infestation. There are two principal molecules in conifers: pinene, which has a piney odor, and limonene, which has more of a citrusy smell. Any combination of these two molecules, among some others, gives conifer trees their distinctive scent. To truly appreciate the variety of scents, why not create some conifer scent pouches? Here is how:

- Find 5 or 6 small cotton pouches. Failing that, clean white cotton socks will also work.
- Fill each pouch with small snippets of the needles from one kind of conifer, for example, balsam fir. Make sure you cut the needles into small bits and stuff your pouch until it is almost full. Always think about harvesting honorably, taking just a small amount from one place and then moving on to the next. Try to find at least four or five of the following: cedar, spruce, pine, hemlock, larch, and tamarack. What tree species you find will depend on where you live.

Smelling flowers

Credit: iStock.

AROMATHERAPY

When feeling stressed or overwhelmed, when feeling sick or just not ourselves, we often take a pill to alleviate our symptoms. But a deep breath of the scents of a forest or nearby park can also help us feel better. While going for a walk, collect a small handful of pine needles and inhale deeply. Try the same with other conifer needles, such as hemlock, cedar, fir, and spruce. Simply breathing in the compounds released by the needles improves our mood, provides a boost of energy, and helps us to feel present and in the moment. Try smelling flowers in bloom, moss, lichen, freshly dug earth, the bark of a tree, or even the water of pond, lake, or stream. When breathing in these odors, we are literally taking a part of nature deep into ourselves through the chemical compounds that are released. The sense of smell is one of the most powerful and ancient connectors of all.

Cecropia moth

Credit: Pixabay.

PHERMONIA

A female cecropia moth releases pheromones (special chemicals) that, amazingly, attract a male moth from up to 1.9 miles (3 kilometers) away. The male's feathery antennae can, just like a beacon, hone in on the female's location by scent alone. Other silk moths (Polyphemus, Promethea, and Luna moths) use this same strategy.

Scent Trail Activity

- Fill Mason jars ⅓ of the way with sand. Purchase incense. Try to find 4 or 5 different natural scents (for example: sage, juniper, pine, red cedar).
- Trim the incense stick so that it is shorter than the jar. Place one lit incense stick in the middle at the bottom of each jar.
- Light the incense. Hide a variety of these jars, each with a different scent, along a trail. Just like moths, can people hone in on the scent? Can they recognize the smell?

Smell Scavenger Hunt

There are so many different kinds of natural aromas out there. From the tangy smell of pine to the moist and earthy smell of moss; from the lemony smell of citronella ants (yes they exist!), to the minty smell of wintergreen, nature is replete with a wide variety of odours. We can train our noses to be more sensitive to the palette of smells of every place.

Here is an activity that helps you cue into the symphony of smells that exists right outside your door.

Copy the Smell Scavenger Hunt located on page 78. Can you find smells that match the photo? How many distinctive smells can you find?

SMELL SCAVENGER HUNT

	WHAT I FOUND THAT SMELLS LIKE THIS...
1. EARTHY →	
2. LEMONY →	
3. FRUITY →	
4. MOSSY →	
5. MOIST →	
6. MINTY →	
7. PINEY →	
8. FLOWERY →	
9. GRASSY →	

Credit: photos Pixabay, design David Lindblad.

SEASONAL SMELL ACTIVITIES

- Note how each season has its own distinctive smell-scape. For example, in spring you might notice the grassy smell of a freshly mowed lawn, the fragrant aroma of lilac, or the pungent scent of freshly turned soil.

- In summer, you might detect the fresh salty smell of the ocean or the moist scent of a pond, river, or lake. You might take in the sweet aroma of summer hay.

- In autumn, the distinctive and earthy smell of leaves on a lawn or park. You might notice a fresher, sharper smell carried by the autumn winds.

- In winter, there may be a sharpness that causes a tingling in your nose due to the drier, colder winter air. Can you smell snow or ice? Every place has its own seasonal smell-scape. Tune into and notice yours as each season passes.

THE WORLD OF TOUCH

WE ARE ENVELOPED in our skin. It is what protects us from the rest of the world, from harmful radiation, from insect bites, from cold, from heat, from sharp objects, and from a host of parasites and diseases. Our skin is the median through which we are connected to everything else. It is what contains us and makes each of us unique. Our skin is how we make contact with everything around us. We are always touching something—the chair you are sitting on, the air brushing against your face, your hand resting on the table—we continually receive tactile information about the world around us.

Our skin is our largest sensory organ. And it has some miraculous qualities. Our skin can mend itself if torn or punctured. It is always renewing itself; it cools us down on hot days and warms us up on cold days. It is washable, flexible, and waterproof. And it comes in a variety of different forms—hair, nails, soft skin; or if you are a mammal, bird, or lizard—claws, spines, feathers, scales, and whiskers.

Your skin has several layers, like an onion. The very top layer is called the epidermis and serves as your body's protective coating, your built-in skin jacket. This outer layer contains melanin which gives your skin its unique color and protects you from harmful UV radiation. In fact, the more sun there is, the more you'll make melanin and the darker your skin becomes. The next layer down is your dermis, which contain your sweat glands, oil glands, hair follicles, nerve endings, and touch receptors. Below the dermis, you have a bottom layer composed of connective tissue and fat cells. The fatty layer not only insulates you on those cold January days but also helps protect the tissue underneath from your brother's fist, or from falling down the stairs. And, of course, the connective tissue connects muscles and tendons to your skin.

OUR SOMATOSENSORY SYSTEM

Our sense of touch is regulated by the somatosensory system, composed of nerve endings and touch receptors. Anything we feel—from pain to itchiness, from smooth to rough, from hot to cold—is controlled by this system.

Helping us to sense vibrations, pressure, and textures are our mechanoreceptors. Crammed throughout the ridges of your fingertips are Meissner's corpuscles, en-abling you to detect even the gentlest of touches. Stroke the tip of a feather or leaf against your fingertips and you'll see it takes only the slightest of pressure to feel its presence. Your lips and tongue are also equally sensitive (as you'll know if you've kissed a loved one), as are your eyelids, face, and the soles of your feet. Deeper down in the dermis, among your tendons, muscles, and joints, are Pacinian corpuscles and

Diagram of sense of touch

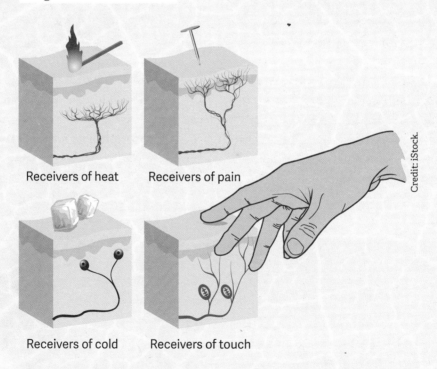

Receivers of heat   Receivers of pain

Receivers of cold   Receivers of touch

Credit: iStock.

Ruffini's corpuscles. These receptors help you to sense the movement of your limbs and where your body is in space and time, so you can catch a ball, skip rope, or sit yourself down in a chair.

You also have hot and cold thermoreceptors, found in the dermis layer of your skin, that enable you to sense different temperatures. Cold receptors begin to warn you when the temperature of the surface of your skin falls below 95°F (35°C). They are particularly active when your skin temperature drops below 77°F (25°C) and begin to shut down at temperatures below 41°F (5°C). This explains why your fingers and toes begin to lose feeling when they are extremely cold.

You begin to feel hot when the surface of your skin rises to 86°F (30°C). You feel the hottest when the temperature rises to around 113°F (45°C). After this, your pain receptors kick in so that you are motivated to find a cooler place. Interestingly, while there are thermoreceptors all over your body, there are greater concentrations of cold receptors than hot receptors. You have an abundance of thermoreceptors in your ears, face, and nose—which is why these areas always seem to get cold first.

With over 3 million pain receptors throughout the tissues of your body—in your muscles, skin, some organs, and even your bones—pain helps you react immediately to stimuli such as cuts, burns, scrapes, or stings. There are even receptors that create a dull pain to prevent you from using part of your body that has been injured, whether it is a sprain or a broken collarbone, until it heals.

All of these receptors transmit signals to the brain via specialized nerve cells. For example, if your hand touches a hot stove, both mechanical and pain receptors send a message to the brain causing you to suddenly pull your hand away. It is this same system that helps you to delight in the soft caress of a puppy's fur, or the warmth of sunlight brushing against your cheek, or the feel of cool water on a hot day. It is this system that literally puts us in touch with the natural world.

BLINDFOLD ACTIVITIES

Feely Blanket/Feely Bags

When we take the time to feel something, we often do so with our eyes open. But just by closing our eyes and isolating our sense of touch, we can experience nature in an entirely new way.

For this activity, collect a series of objects: interestingly shaped sticks, different rocks with rough and smooth textures, shells, bones, feathers, pinecones, leaves, grasses.

- Place items under a blanket, along the periphery.
- Have participants lie down on their stomachs and ask them to slide their hands under the blanket. By using their sense of touch, can they guess what lies underneath? Ask participants periodically to scooch over so that everyone has an opportunity to feel each of the objects.
- As an alternative (and this seems to work well for younger children), place a variety of natural objects inside an old pillowcase. Place smooth objects in one, rougher in another. No peeking!

Feely bag

Credit: Jacob Rodenburg.

Blindfold Trail

For this activity you'll need a long rope 150 feet (50 meters) or so.

- Find a trail through a natural area that is free of trash and hazardous objects. If you can, select a portion of the trail that goes through both woods and field. Make sure the ground is fairly even.
- Stretch the rope so that it follows along the trail. Try tying it to interesting stopping points, perhaps an old trunk, an interestingly shaped rock, an area with soft grass. Blindfold your participants.
- If you feel comfortable and there aren't sharp rocks or sticks, ask participants to remove one shoe and sock. Please scout this area carefully first before you go barefoot.
- Start in a line and have the participants walk slowly, running their hands along the rope and following where the rope trail takes them. Tell them to touch objects (the ground, the rocks, the trees). Have them sweep their hands along tall grasses, feeling the texture of the seed heads.
- Ask them to sit in a soft spot along the way. Can they feel the wind against their cheeks? Can they notice the temperature change as they walk from open areas to shady areas?
- When they complete the trail, have participants remove their blindfolds and walk along it with their eyes open. How do both experiences compare?

CONNECTING TO EARTH

We are powerfully connected to the earth when we are in touch (literally) with the earth itself. When we feel our skin against the soil, the living matrix that gives rise to life on land, we are linking up with the very life systems that support and nurture us.

Earthing

Some people practice "earthing." They believe that the electrical energy arising out of the earth, when it touches their body, is actually healing. They walk barefoot, they lie directly on the earth, or they cover their bodies with soil. People who do this regularly say that they sleep better, their mood improves, and they feel healthier. As small children, perhaps we instinctively knew this. Remember how you enjoyed the feeling of mud against your skin? And more than one exasperated parent has hosed down their child, murmuring "why, why, why oh why?" There is a good reason why kids and some adults love soil and mud. Mud just makes us happier. It turns out that soil contains a bacteria called Mycobacterium vaccae, which serves to boost the level of serotonin in our brains. Serotonin is a chemical that helps us feel positive, relaxed, and happy. At the same time, playing in mud strengthens our immune system and helps build resiliency. Perhaps it is time to take a lesson from ourselves when we were children.

Earthing

Credit: iStock.

- Kick your shoes off. Cover your feet with soil and soak in the energy of earth. Feel its coolness and its soothing texture against the soles of your feet. One handful of soil contains more living organisms than all the people on earth. The earth is throbbing with life, and we can feel the potential of growth, resiliency, and renewal coursing up through our skin. It helps us to realize that the answer to many of our problems lies in the regenerative and healing power of nature.

Mud Pies

No, you are never too old to make mud pies. It is wonderful to make something that looks delicious and not feel obliged to eat it. So, delight in the gifts of the earth and make mud pies!

- Take an aluminum pie plate and fill this with gooey mud. Decorate the top with flowers, twigs, leaves, and stones. Make imprints by pressing something with texture into the soft mud and carefully removing it. Try using shells, conifer cones, and leaves. Leave to dry and admire your work!

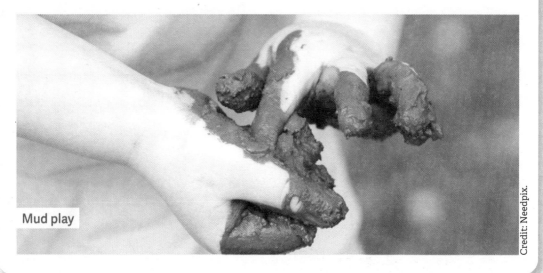

Mud play

Credit: Needpix.

CONNECTING TO TREES

My Personal Friend

Here is a fun activity that can work in a park, school ground, or backyard.

- You'll need a blindfold and participants divided into pairs. Demonstrate how the activity works first. Select a volunteer and gently blindfold them. Tell them that they are going to meet one of your special friends. Turn them about several times and then begin to walk in a circuitous route towards an interesting tree. Try to select a tree with low-hanging leaves and twigs.
- Have your volunteer meet the tree. Shake its "hand" by feeling a leaf on the branch. Ask them to run their hands along the contour of the leaf.
  - Are the edges serrated (toothed) or smooth? Are they lobed (curved) or straight? Perhaps the tree is a conifer (cone-bearing with needles)? If so, what do the needles feel like?
  - If you've selected a deciduous tree (the kind that loses its leaves), what is the pattern of the veining under the leaf? Is it palmate (coming from one central spot) or parallel (arranged in parallel lines along a central vein)?
  - How are the branches arranged on the tree? Are they opposite each other or alternate?
  - What does the bark feel like? Smooth or rough?
  - Does the tree have a special smell? Each of these is a clue that helps your volunteer determine what kind of tree it is.
  - Feel around the base of tree. Any neighbors? Are there distinctive holes?
- When your volunteer has become thoroughly acquainted with their newfound friend, take them back to where they started. But don't go in a straight line. Wander a bit.
- Lastly spin them a few times. Take off their blindfold. Now, using their eyes, can they find their friend? It is harder than it sounds!

Now that you've shown how this activity works, encourage the rest of the group to give it a try.

Hug a Tree

Tree huggers have acquired a certain stereotype. They are often imagined in sandals, sporting a beard, with a bag of granola close at hand and exuding an earthy odor. And it is easy to dismiss tree hugging as a silly and an esoteric pastime. But there is something so nourishing and calming when you wrap your arms around a tree and squeeze tight. When you feel the texture of the bark against your chest and cheek and imagine this gentle giant being, with its roots extending throughout the soil, you too begin to experience a sense of grounding and rootedness.

- Go and find a nearby tree, one that you can almost fully encircle with your arms. Press your body along its trunk and nestle your cheek up against its bark. Close your eyes and imagine. Imagine that, on a sunny day, this being is transpiring over 3,000 liters of water into the air, moistening and cooling the surrounding environment.
- Imagine how this tree's roots, hundreds of kilometers of them, are spreading out, seeking nutrients and water. The roots then send these upward through the trunk at speeds

My personal friend

Credit: iStock.

of almost 62 miles (100 kilometers) an hour on a sunny day!

- Imagine the roots reaching out and caressing other roots from other trees, exchanging chemical signals through the mycelium network. Roots are encased in a fungal network of mycelium. Imagine this beautiful relationship. The mycelium borrows sugars from the largest "hub" trees that produce more food than they need. In exchange, the mycelium helps absorb water and nutrients for the tree to use.

- Imagine these trees talking to each other through the "wood wide web." When one tree is being attacked by insects or disease, it will let the other tree know by releasing a chemical signal, providing an opportunity for trees to mount a defence.

- As you hug your tree, look up into the canopy. Those leaves swaying in the wind are doing something incredible. Take one hand and grab a handful of sunlight. Don't let it slip through your fingers! Now cram it in your mouth and chew. That is what you call a "light" snack! OK, humans can't eat sunlight, but in a way, trees can. Like all plants, they produce sugars from water, carbon dioxide, and sunlight in a process known as photosynthesis.

- Take a deep breath in. And quietly offer gratitude to the tree that you are hugging. For that tree is providing you and other living things with oxygen. Two mature trees can provide enough oxygen for a family of four to survive!

- Now breathe out. You are releasing carbon dioxide, exactly what the tree needs, along with sunlight and water to make its own food. What a cool arrangement! What you don't need (carbon dioxide), the tree needs, and what the tree doesn't need (oxygen), you do.

- Imagine, as you hug this tree, all the gifts this being is bestowing upon the land it is situated on. Just by being there, your tree is doing more good than harm. It uptakes carbon (and during this time of climate change, that is a special gift indeed), it gives oxygen, it cools and freshens the air, its roots anchor and aerate the soil, and it provides food and habitat for other living things. Imagine if we were all a bit more like the very tree you are hugging. And just imagine that, like your tree, we learn to give more than we take, that we learn to do more good than harm. Now that is worth a hug!

What is Needling You?

- Gather a small sprig of as many of the following as you can: white or western cedar, various pines (white pine, red pine, longleaf pine, jack pine, pitch pine), fir, hemlock, or any other conifer growing in your area. Remember a conifer simply means a tree that has needles and cones.
- Stick each sprig you gathered into a clean sock, far down into the toe so it can't be seen. You should have a variety of socks, each with their own conifer sprig tucked at the bottom.
- If you can, print a color photo of each conifer sprig. Place these photos on the ground.
- Now ask participants to stick their hands into each sock and, using their sense of touch, attempt to match the sprig to the photo. You'll be surprised at the variety of needle shapes and sizes.
- As a complementary activity, place different sprigs into a small canister and have participants smell each. Note the different scents (see scratch and sniff, page 71).

Get the Point

Here are some needle characteristics and a few mnemonics that will help you identify them.

- Spruce needles spiral along the branch and are sharp like spikes, so they are painful to the touch. Because they are rounded, they roll or spin between your thumb and finger.
- Fir needles are flat and very flexible. They don't roll!
- Pine needles are usually very long like pins. White pine, a common species in the East, has the same number of needles as the number of letters in the word "white," namely five.
- Cedars have scale-like flattened leaves, just like fish that live in the sea! ("sea"dar).
- Hemlock needles are very small, green on top, and appear white underneath. To connect the needles to the word "hemlock," think of the prefix "hemi," which means "half." Hemlock needles are half white and half green.
- Junipers have two types of leaves (often on the same tree): small

scale-like leaves, similar to those of a cedar, as well as longer (¼ in / 6 mm) dark blue-green needle-like leaves. Think of a pair of different leaves and "juni-pair."

- Larches or tamaracks are leafless in winter. The rest of the year, they have tufts of up to 20 very soft, limp needles.

Touch Scavenger Hunt

As you walk through a forest or field, just gently touch the natural objects around you. Can you feel the textures on the Touch Scavenger Hunt sheet?

TOUCH SCAVENGER HUNT

WHAT I FOUND THAT FEELS LIKE THIS...

1. MOIST →
2. COOL →
3. FUZZY →
4. SILKY →
5. LIGHT →
6. SOFT →
7. SMOOTH →
8. SHARP →

Credit: photos Pixabay; design by David Lindblad.

The Book of Nature Connection Worksheets are available for free download at: https://newsociety.com/pages/book-of-nature-connection-worksheets

OTHER TOUCH ACTIVITIES

Touch Gardens

Children love to touch the world. They are exploring the delightful textures of smoothness, roughness, tenderness, and hardness—through their sensitive fingertips. A touch garden is a great way for them to literally shake the hands of nature. Each of these plants listed below, have a distinctive feel. During the spring, plant a small box garden with the following recommended plants for a touch garden:

sunflower	pussy willow
lamb's ears	woolly thyme
dandelion	wormwood
Jerusalem sage	chenille
mullein	allium
common milkweed	passionflower
nasturtium	sedum autumn fire
rhubarb	hyacinth
coneflower	feather grass
amaranth	snapdragons
lily poppy	

You can also gather small samples of many of these and place them in a feely bag (see page 84).

Invite children (and adults too) to rub the leaves of each of these plants. Ask them to really feel the texture of each plant. Which one felt the nicest? Which one felt uncomfortable? What does the texture of the plant tell us about its properties? A thick and prickly leaf like a cactus helps to store water and protect the plant. A smooth leaf grows more quickly. A heavily veined leaf provides more support. Leaves end at a point so they can shed water. Pine needles have evolved to be waxy and thick in order to reduce water loss, especially in winter. Complex edges and lobes allow leaves to get rid of absorbed heat very rapidly; smooth edges are more common in shade-loving plants because getting rid of heat is not as much of a problem.

TASTING THE WORLD

SOMETHING ALWAYS tastes better when it is shared. A home-cooked meal says that I care about you and I want your hunger to be satisfied in a way that you will enjoy and savor. Serving tea and scones in a group invites conversation. Cold beer or a glass of wine makes you and your friends feel relaxed. A freshly baked cookie placed in our hand helps us forget about the troubles of the moment as we delight in the sweet and doughy texture in our mouths. When someone does something we approve of and admire, we say that person has good taste. We often use the descriptors of taste to describe how we feel. We might encounter the bitterness of love gone wrong, experience the sweet taste of victory, or perhaps we've even done something tasteless.

The link between emotion and taste isn't an accident—taste was the very thing that ensured our survival. Thousands of years ago, a very bitter or sour taste may have indicated that the food we were eating was poisonous. Something with a salty or sweet taste may have indicated that food was packed full of nutrients. A savory taste meant that the food was rich in protein. Paying attention to the taste of our food and having good taste was literally a means of survival.

Crammed in our mouths like tiny volcanoes are taste buds, some 10,000 of them, that are organized around the type of taste they help to detect (sweet, salty, bitter, and sour). There is even one called umami that detects savory flavors. Each taste bud in turn has about 50 to 100 taste cells, and each cell has receptors that bind to certain molecules that give rise to the sensation of sweet, salty, bitter, and umami. Taste cells mound together to create a kind of a capsule that has a pore on top. The pore contains long, slender sensory cells known as taste hairs. Proteins on the surface of these hairs trigger sensory neurons that transmit this information to four areas in the brain, and voila, we experience the sense of taste.

What we detect as "taste" is actually a combination of sensations—not just what is sensed by the tongue but the sense of taste also involves the texture, temperature, and smell of what we are eating. We only truly taste after we smell our food. You might have noticed that you don't taste as much if you are suffering from a plugged nose and a cold.

The following activities will help you explore various tastes in nature.

Basic Tastes

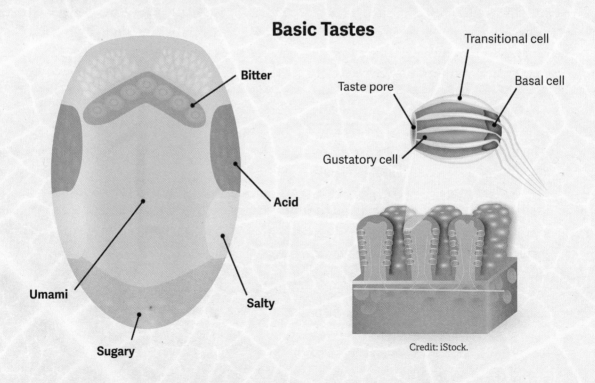

Credit: iStock.

THE EDIBLE WILD

One of my favorite quotes comes from Aldo Leapold who once said: "The healthiest food is the shortest distance from the earth to your mouth."

There is something so energizing about eating the food you find. The flavors from the wild are powerful connectors to nature.

It goes without saying that we have to be so careful when it comes to harvesting and eating from the wild. It is especially true when it comes to young children who are tempted to plop everything into their mouths. This is their way of making "sense" of the world around them by using their sense of taste. I remember walking along a beach with my daughter, who was two years old at the time. I noticed she would periodically hunch down and grab something from the ground. She would squeeze out green sludge from between her fingers, and then she'd gleefully lick it. Being a bit concerned, I ran back to investigate. It turns out she was eating goose poop! In that instance, I wasn't entirely sure if my daughter was developing good taste!

So, a word of caution…please use your judgement. There are so many wonderful flavors to be found in the forest and fields. But make sure you know exactly what it is that you are eating, before you serve it! Here are few tried-and-true flavors that are difficult to get wrong.

Pine and Cedar Tea

As you walk, harvest a handful of eastern white cedar (the needles look a bit like feathers) and white pine (long soft needles in bunches of 5). When you get home, toss these in boiling water and let steep for at least 5 minutes. The resulting tea will be bitter but refreshing, and your tongue will dance with a pungent but evocative taste of the forest! It is always best practice when harvesting from the wild to take just a bit of what you've harvested, to gauge your body's reaction. So, try a small cup of tea to start.

Pine tea

Credit: iStock.

Cattails

Found across most of North America, cattails are a very common plant of wetlands, ditches, moist fields, and thickets. One of the most distinguishing features is the cigar-like head atop a round stalk that is 5 feet (1.5 meters) to 10 feet (3 meters) tall. Known as "candlewicks," these brown tightly packed seed heads contain thousands of tiny, fluffy seed. If ever you are lost, break apart these seed packages and use the fluffy heads to insulate your core. You can also use the inside drier seeds as a tinder to start a fire. The leaves are long and slender and are attached to the bottom of the plant. The lower younger, and more tender leaves can be used in a salad. The lower inside pith of the cattail can be eaten raw or chopped up and used in a stir-fry. Be careful, however. Because cattails absorb toxins from the water, be sure that you are harvesting cattails in an area that has clean water.

Cattails

Credit: Pixabay.

Wintergreen

Here is an opportunity to freshen your breath and taste the minty, earthy flavor of the forest. You can recognize wintergreen by its thick leathery leaves that stay green even in winter. Wintergreen (also known as boxberry, teaberry, mountain tea, or checkerberry) can be found both in Canada (from Manitoba to the Maritime Provinces) and throughout the eastern half of the United States as far south as Alabama. Growing low to the ground, the leaf edges are smooth and the surface is shiny. Rub a wintergreen leaf vigorously between your fingers to release the fragrant oils. Often a quick rub and sniff will release a strong wintergreen scent. If you are sure it is wintergreen, place a leaf in your mouth and chew slowly. It may take a while, but the flavor will slowly seep out and spread the mintilicious taste throughout your mouth. Spit out the leaf bits. And take only one leaf, though, for ingesting too many leaves can be hard on the stomach. And take a deep breath in. You might be transported back to your childhood, remembering your grandmother's mints hidden at the bottom of her purse, or you may recall the freshness of Wint-O-Green LifeSavers that were so popular many years ago.

Wintergreen leaves contain methyl salicylate, which often used as an ingredient in pain-relief ointments. In some traditional Indigenous cultures, a poultice or a tea was made out of crushed leaves as way to ease pain.

Lots of animals love to browse wintergreen. The berries are bright red and are edible as well. Turkey, deer, grouse, mice, and even bears have been known to include wintergreen in their diets, especially during winter.

Wintergreen

Credit: Pixabay.

Dandelion

How fortunate that one of our most common plants is edible. And while some people consider this a weed, dandelion is a powerhouse when it comes to the edible wild. Most of us recognize the toothy leaves (the name itself is French for "lion's teeth") and the bright yellow flower. It is a splash of sunshine and happiness on an otherwise green expanse of lawn. How sad that not everyone views dandelions in this way. Here are a few cautionary notes about harvesting dandelions:

- Don't harvest dandelions near roads of from an industrial site—they can absorb toxins.
- Don't harvest dandelions from a yard where fertilizers or pesticides have been used.

Select an area where there is little sun exposure and harvest the newest young leaves. These are the least bitter. You can use dandelion leaves in salad. The best come from plants that haven't flowered yet. Even older leaves are palatable providing you remove the mid-vein and boil them in two changes of water. The cooked leaves contain more nutrients than spinach. The unopened flower buds can be used in salads or cooked in a stir-fry. You can even make dandelion flower fritters. Just remove the green base of the flower, which can be quite bitter, and dip into a batter made from eggs, flour, and milk. Fry these up, drain away the oil, and enjoy!

Try harvesting the roots and roasting them. They make a tasty coffee substitute. The best time to harvest the roots is before the plant has flowered. Remove the smaller hairier roots and chop up the larger ones into chunks. Roast on a pan at 350°F for 40 minutes. Boil the roasted roots in water with cinnamon and or cardamom. Strain through a sieve, add milk, and serve.

Dandelion

Credit: Pixabay.

TASTES OF THE SEASON

Almost anywhere and anytime, we can shop for an orange from South Africa, curry from India, or bananas from the Caribbean. And while it is wonderful to have this range of choice, it does come at a cost. For example, consider the carbon emitted from the energy it took to transport produce from around the world, on ships, on trucks, and on trains. Also, consider the water it took to irrigate the fields, the energy it took to make the fertilizers, and the pesticides used to make sure there was an abundant harvest. There aren't easy answers for how to create a just global food system that provides people with work, a fair wage, and is sustainable. It may help if we eat more locally and in season. There are so many wonderful tastes that are arriving each and every month, from the fresh berries and herbs of spring to the wonderful fruits and vegetables of fall and winter—think about root vegetables like turnips and greens like kale. Don't forget to visit your local farmers market and explore what vegetables and fruits are in season.

Kale

Credit: Pixabay.

GRATITUDE FOR NATURE

In a consumer-driven culture where everyone is pressured to buy ever more, and where our happiness seems dependent on how much wealth we accumulate, we aren't often asked, nor do we take the opportunity, to give thanks. And yet there is so much to be grateful for. From the fresh air we breathe to the water that quenches our thirst, from the plants that provide oxygen and food to the insects that pollinate our flowers, from the trees that moisten our air to the rivers and lakes that provide fish and so much more. An attitude of gratitude for nature and its many gifts is a conscious act that helps us recognize that we do not exist as singular beings but rather that we are embedded in a wonderful interconnected system that supports and nourishes us all. Practicing gratitude reminds us that we too have an obligation to nurture, support, and give thanks that we exist in connection with so many other beings, with our ancestors and those yet to come. And if at the same time, we take the effort to practice reciprocity, by giving something back, this small gesture may help our words of thanks carry extra meaning out into the world.

Pass out this Gratitude Card to your participants.

Gratitude Card	Suggested Words of Thanks
Sun	Thank you, Sun, for flooding the world with your brightness, your energy, and your warmth. Without you, no plants could grow, there would be no food for us, nor for our winged, footed, swimming, and crawling friends. Without you, the world would be a cold and lonely place. For all your gifts, I give thanks.
Soil	Thank you, Soil, for the magic and fertile bed that allows plants to take root, to grow, and to flourish. You have given rise to the plant world that provides us and other living things with food, shelter, and oxygen. Without you, the world would be a barren and desolate place. For all your gifts, I give thanks.
Trees	Thank you, Trees, for your beauty, strength, and steadfastness. Your arching canopy gives shade. Your leaves uptake carbon, give oxygen, and provide shelter and food. Your roots anchor the soil and prevent erosion. You provide homes for countless animals, birds, and insects. You whisper and sing to me in the wind. For all your gifts, I give thanks.
Birds	Thank you, Birds, for your winged beauty, for your soaring springtime songs, and for your elegant color and form. You make my walks joyful. I admire your diversity, your ability to hide among the plant world, and your diligence as you gather food and care for your young. For all your gifts, I give thanks.
Wildflowers	Thank you, Wildflowers, for your beautiful palette of colors, for your cheerfulness, and for your hardiness. Even in the winter, your seed heads burst with the promise of new life. Thank you for your blossoms heavy with nectar and pollen that provide food for the many insects that have come to depend on you. For all your gifts, I give thanks.
Insects	To the Butterflies and Moths whose wings flash in such an amazing array of colors, patterns, and shapes. To the bees who work so hard to pollinate, to the ants who work cooperatively with the dedication and commitment that we envy, to the dragonflies that dart about with stealth and quickness, to the mosquitoes that provide food for birds and bats, and the many kinds of beetles that add color to our world. For this and more, I give thanks.
Water	Most of our bodies and most of the world are made of water. It is the liquid of life. To Water, who can tumble over rocks in a frothing torrent, who can hold the color blue in a lake or ocean unlike anything else. To water, whose form can change from rain to a frozen puddle, from a hexagonal snowflake to a glacier, from a dancing stream to a deep ocean—we thank you, Water, for bringing life to us and all living things.
Animals	To the furry four-legged Animals that scurry about the forest. To the legless ones that wind among the grasses, to those that hop, to those that run with strength and grace, to those that swim above and below our rivers, lakes and oceans—we give thanks to you for your beauty and for helping us to bear witness to the wonder all around us.

Seed Gratitude Balls

Here's a recipe for making seed gratitude balls. Use local native seeds collected from your own garden, a seed exchange, or your local garden supply store. Make sure they are suited to the habitat you'll be visiting.

Ingredients

1 cup seeds

5 cups compost (peat-free is best)

2 cups clay powder (available in craft shops) or local clay

water

Directions

1. In a large bowl, mix together approximately 1 cup of native seeds with 5 cups of pure compost and 2 cups of clay powder or local clay.

2. Add water slowly as you mix everything up with your hands until you have a sticky mixture. It should hold a ball shape.

3. Roll the mixture into balls about 1 inch in diameter.

4. Leave your seed gratitude balls to dry in a sunny spot.

Give each participant several seed gratitude balls. Have them look at every part of nature and even touch (if possible) that which they are thanking. Ask them to either read the suggested words of thanks or create their own expressions of gratitude. After everyone has spoken, have them gently place their seed ball next to what they are thanking, as an expression of gratitude and reciprocity.

SOME POSSIBLE SEEDS to include for open areas are bee balm (Mondara fistulosa), purple coneflower (Echinacea purpurea), New England aster (Symphyotrichum laeve), common milkweed (Asclepia syriaca), brown-eyed Susan (Rudbeckia triloba).

When collecting seeds for a forest, in the fall, find cones from evergreens (pine, cedar, spruce, hemlock, fir—whatever is growing in your area). Place on a paper towel and allow them to dry out for several months. After they have dried, tap the cones gently and the seeds should fall out. Place these in a paper envelope and label them. Store until spring. You can either plant these directly into the soil or place them in your seed gratitude ball.

SENSORY WALKS

While this book has provided you with a wide variety of sensory activities, they are organized around each sense. Here are some suggested ways for you to put them together to create an engaging sensory hike.

Forest Walks

Stop 1: *Nature Mindfulness* (page 5) — Ask participants to find a quiet spot and sit, while you review the hints of practicing mindfulness. This encourages participants to be present in this moment.

As you walk (page 8): Use *focused hearing* to really listen to forest sounds.

Stop 2: *Holmsing the Leaf* (page 66)— To foster observation, curiosity and wonder.

As you walk (page 26): *Practice stalking.*

Stop 3: *My Personal Friend* (page 88)— To appreciate the individual character of each tree.

As you walk: *Smell Cocktail* (page 71)—To appreciate the variety of aromas in a forest.

Stop 4: *Poetree* (page 53)—To highlight the connection between participants and a tree and to encourage creative thought and imagination.

At the same spot: *Tree Songs* (page 14)—To savor the sound of wind through different trees. Also: *Hug a Tree* (page 89)—Take the time to really savor the gifts of a tree.

As you walk: *Touch Scavenger Hunt* (page 92)—To appreciate the variety of textures in a forest.

Stop 5: *Framing Nature* (page 49)—To isolate certain parts of the forest as way to gain a new perspective .

As you walk: *Seasonal Color Wheel* (page 40)—To appreciate the wide variety of hues associated with the season.

Stop 6: *Micro-trails* (page 59)— To appreciate the very small.

As you walk: *Splatter vision* (page 58)—to help you expand your field of vision and to hone your observation skills.

Stop 7: *Bird Whispering* (page 16)— To notice the beautiful but sometimes elusive birds that are hidden in the forest but not always seen.

As you walk: *Shape Scavenger Hunt* (page 63)—To appreciate the organic shapes and forms of a forest.

Last Stop: *Pine and Cedar Tea* (page 97)—To savor the taste of the forest. Bring along a thermos of very hot water (and enough cups). Add a handful of cedar and/or pine needles 5 minutes before you serve. Add a smidgen of honey or maple syrup.

City Park Walks

Stop 1: *Nature Mindfulness* **(page 5)**—Ask participants to find a quiet spot and sit, while you review the hints of practicing mindfulness. This encourages participants to be present in this moment.

As you walk: *Blindfold Trail* **(page 85)**—To tune into the temperature variations, the different textures and feel of a park underfoot (only remove shoes if it is safe to do so. Please scout this area in advance).

Stop 2: *Scent Trails* **(page 72)**—To appreciate the remarkable sensory abilities of animals in an urban park.

As you walk: *Scratch and Sniff* **(page 71)**—To savor the wide variety of scents in a forest.

Stop 3: *Feely Blanket/Feely Bags* **(page 84)**—To appreciate the diversity of textures and forms in an urban park.

As you walk: *Shape Scavenger Hunt* **(page 63)**—To highlight the organic forms and shapes of natural objects in an urban park.

Stop 4: *Nature Sculpting* **(page 48)**—Creating beautiful art using material found in nature helps us appreciate the natural world in new ways.

As you walk: *Fingers Up* **(page 21)**—How many distinctive nature sounds could you hear?

Stop 5: *Nature Music* **(page 31)**—To focus on the different sounds natural material can make. Using creativity to create musical pieces helps us appreciate nature in new ways.

As you walk: *Camouflaged Animals* **(page 44)**—Hide your animals along the way. Use this as an opportunity to talk about the ways in which animals use and depend on camouflage.

Stop 6:—*Basement Windows* **(page 54)**—To appreciate the unique life forms that often remains hidden from our eyes.

As you walk: *Splatter vision* **(page 58)**—To expand your field of vision and help you to hone your observation skills.

Stop 7: *The Lost Game* **(page 112)**—To appreciate how important our sense of direction is.

Backyard/Confined Spaces Activities

Micro Trails (page 59)—To appreciate the very small.

Human Camera (page 60)—To see the world in a unique way.

Framing Nature (page 49)—By isolating a part of nature, we gain a new perspective.

Seasonal Color Scavenger Hunt (page 38)—Appreciating the hues of the season.

Camouflaged Animals/Camouflaged Eggs (page 44/46)—Explore ways in which animals use and depend on camouflage.

Scent Pouches (page 73)—To focus on the variety of unique smells found in nature.

Scent Scavenger Hunt (page 77)—So you can appreciate the wide variety of natural scents that are close by.

Earthing (page 86)—To directly connect to the Earth.

Mud Pies (page 87)—To be creative and develop a sense of fun and playfulness in nature.

Feely Blanket/Feely Bags (page 84)—To appreciate the unique textures and forms found in nature.

Taste of the Season (page 101)—Try a picnic featuring seasonal foods. Can you garnish this with something found in your backyard or garden (see pages 97–100 for ideas).

Reflection Questions

- Did this experience help you appreciate the forest in new ways?
- Do you feel calmer, more grounded, at peace?
- Which of these activities might you do again?
- Which of these activities was the most evocative for you?
- Do you feel more connected to the natural world around you?
- Does it make you feel motivated to protect these special places from threats such as habitat loss and climate change?

OTHER SENSES

There are of course other senses, and exactly what they are is still up for debate. One that most scientists agree with is called proprioception, or how your brain interprets where your body is in time and space. You have proprioceptors located in your joints, muscles, and tendons that sense where certain body parts are in relation to each other. These receptors detect muscle length and tension, helping you to perform the most basic tasks such as balancing, walking, sitting, and eating.

SENSE OF DIRECTION

With your eyes closed, try touching the tip of your nose with your finger. Imagine walking along a rocky trail but your body maintains its balance, even while stepping along a constantly shifting landscape. Mechanosensation helps us detect pressure, but some people have a mutated gene that interferes with their ability to detect touch or limb movement. We use proprioception to figure out where we are. Here is a game that helps you appreciate the importance of your sense of direction.

The Lost Game

In a large field, place a pylon about 300 feet (100 meters) away (if you don't have the room, less than 300 feet (100 meters) will also work).

- Blindfold a participant, point them in the direction of the pylon.
- Ask them to walk toward the pylon and to stop when they feel they've arrived there.
- Observe what happens.

Invariably people begin to veer off course, sometimes quite dramatically. It may be because one leg is a bit stronger than the other or that the landscape subtly bounces us off our line. When we don't have reference points, it is so easy to become disoriented. This may be why people lost in the woods, without a clear line of sight, tend to walk in circles.

I remember taking a shortcut while in Yellowknife in the northern reaches of Canada. I wanted to visit a waterfall, but I could not seem to find it. It was wintertime, and the sky was overcast. The temperature began to drop. It was -40°C, and I was cold and rapidly getting colder. Finally, the sun peeked out from behind a cloud. For a moment, I stood in amazement, and in my mind, I said, no—that can't be! The sun is in the wrong spot—it should be over there. Finally, I realized how ridiculous my thinking was, and I was completely turned around. Now having an idea of roughly where I was, I found my way out to a road and continued on home again. To help you know where you are on the land, recognize where the sun is at various times of the day and during different seasons of the year, for your region of the world.

Maintaining a Straight Line

Here's an easy way to keep a straight line if you are lost in the woods.

- From where you are standing, take note of a tree or a landmark right beside you. In the distance, sight another tree or landmark. Make your way there.
- Look back at your previous landmark, where you are currently standing, and select another landmark in the distance, making sure that these three points are all in a straight line.
- If you continue to do this, you'll ensure that you remain more or less on a straight line.

There are other senses you use that you barely notice. There are sensors in your neurons that help you monitor and control the tilt of your head. Others detect movement in your muscles and tendons. Yet others are able to detect the levels of oxygen in your bloodstream in various parts of your body.

Synesthesia

Wouldn't it be amazing if we could hear colors or smell sound? While it seems impossible, some humans are capable of blending two senses. It is called synesthesia, and a person who has this ability is called a synesthete. This remarkable melding of two senses occurs when one sensory pathway to the brain accidentally gives rise to another sensory pathway and the two become linked. In projective synesthesia, when people hear a particular sound, for example the sound of a trumpet, they may see both a color and a shape, say an orange triangle.

While we may not have this ability, why not practice merging your senses? Let's harness our inner synesthete. Perhaps in this way, we can connect even more deeply to this incredible world that we are privileged to be part of. The next time you are in a grove of trees immersed in the color green, really listen: can you feel a sound that resonates with this color? If you stare really hard at the deep blue of a lake or upward into the depth of the sky, can you imagine the sound blue might make? Does the dark and loamy earth conjure up any music for you? Can you smell the color red, can you taste the sound of a rushing river, or can you feel the scent of pine? Let's be open to the way our senses might work together, each serving to enhance the other, so that we feel even more connected to this place and this moment. And we can feel part of all that happened before us and all that is yet to come. We are part of an unfolding—a becoming of this Earth at this time, right here, right now. Can we honor this by mindfully connecting to what surrounds us—not just for us but for our ancestors and those many generations yet to come?

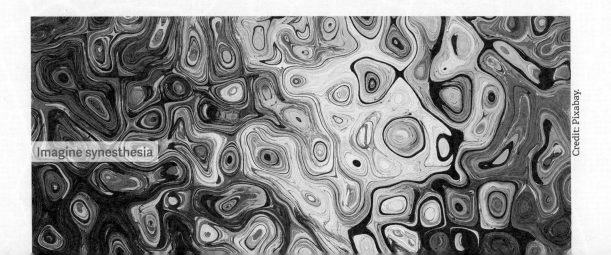
Imagine synesthesia

Credit: Pixabay.

Index of Activities

Index